TO THE READER

This book is presented in its original form and is part of the religious literature and works of Scientology® Founder, L. Ron Hubbard. It is a record of Mr. Hubbard's observations and research into the nature of man and each individual's capabilities as a spiritual being, and is not a statement of claims made by the author, publisher or any Church of Scientology.

Scientology is defined as the study and handling of the spirit in relationship to itself, universes and other life. Thus, the mission of the Church of Scientology is a simple one: to help the individual regain his true nature, as a spiritual being, and thereby attain an awareness of his relationship with his fellow man and the universe. Therein lies the path to personal integrity, trust, enlightenment, and spiritual freedom itself.

Scientology and its forerunner and substudy, Dianetics, as practiced by the Church, address only the "thetan" (spirit), which is senior to the body, and its relationship to and effects on the body. While the Church is free, as all churches are, to engage in spiritual healing, its primary goal is increased spiritual awareness for all. For this reason, neither Scientology nor Dianetics is offered as, nor professes to be physical healing, nor is any claim made to that effect. The Church does not accept individuals who desire treatment of physical or mental illness but, instead, requires a competent medical examination for physical conditions, by qualified specialists, before addressing their spiritual cause.

The Hubbard® Electrometer, or E-Meter, is a religious artifact used in the Church. The E-Meter, by itself, does nothing and is only used by ministers and ministers-in-training, qualified in its use, to help parishioners locate the source of spiritual travail.

The attainment of the benefits and goals of the Scientology religion requires each individual's dedicated participation, as only through one's own efforts can they be achieved.

We hope reading this book is only one step of a personal voyage of discovery into this new and vital world religion.

THIS BOOK BELONGS TO

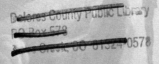

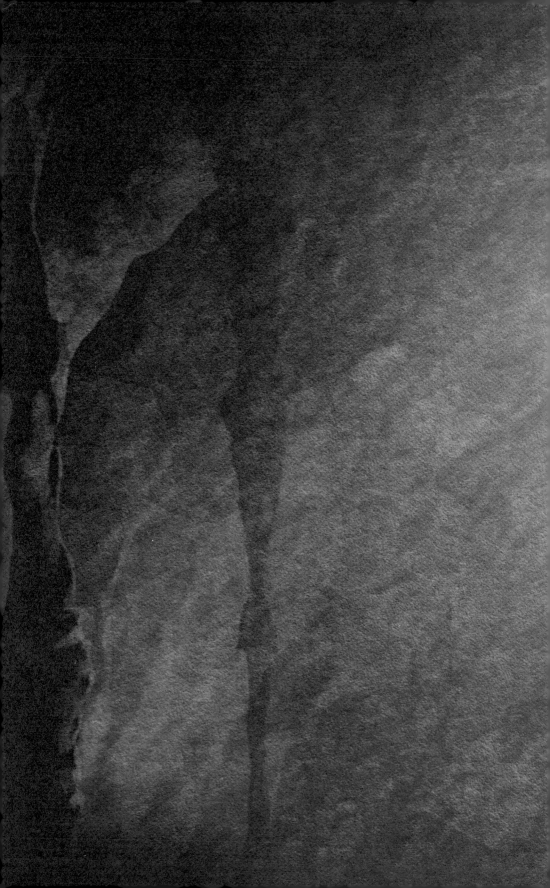

DATE DUE

SCIENTOLOGY
A HISTORY OF
MAN

A LIST AND DESCRIPTION OF THE PRINCIPAL
INCIDENTS TO BE FOUND IN A HUMAN BEING

L. RON HUBBARD

Publications, Inc.

A
HUBBARD®
PUBLICATION

Bridge Publications, Inc.
4751 Fountain Avenue
Los Angeles, California 90029

ISBN 978-1-4031-4423-2

$\mathcal{I}$MPORTANT NOTE

In reading this book, be very certain you never go past a word you do not fully understand. The only reason a person gives up a study or becomes confused or unable to learn is because he or she has gone past a word that was not understood.

The confusion or inability to grasp or learn comes AFTER a word the person did not have defined and understood. It may not only be the new and unusual words you have to look up. Some commonly used words can often be misdefined and so cause confusion.

This datum about not going past an undefined word is the most important fact in the whole subject of study. Every subject you have taken up and abandoned had its words which you failed to get defined.

Therefore, in studying this book be very, very certain you never go past a word you do not fully understand. If the material becomes confusing or you can't seem to grasp it, there will be a word just earlier that you have not understood. Don't go any further, but go back to BEFORE you got into trouble, find the misunderstood word and get it defined.

GLOSSARY

To aid reader comprehension, L. Ron Hubbard directed the editors to provide a glossary. This is included in the Appendix, *Editor's Glossary of Words, Terms and Phrases*. Words sometimes have several meanings. The *Editor's Glossary* only contains the definitions of words as they are used in this text. Other definitions can be found in standard language or Dianetics and Scientology dictionaries.

If you find any other words you do not know, look them up in a good dictionary.

C O N T E N T S

PREFACE

*T*HIS IS TECHNIQUE 88.

Technique 88 is the process of locating the thetan, the "I" of the individual, and the auditing of the thetan.

Technique 88 depends upon a knowledge of Technique 80 which is a mechanical process applicable to any thought or thought mechanism. Tapes on Technique 80* are in the hands of your local organization; the data is being compiled and published as fast as possible.

Technique 88 is an incredible advance over past understanding and obtains incredibly fast results. This does not mean that it is at first glance credible. You will discover that all of it is true as soon as you give it a try.

Technique 88 is an E-Meter technique. You can try 88 without an E-Meter for present life material. An E-Meter is essential for a complete Theta Clearing.

Archimedes, when he discovered how to measure the specific gravity of metals, may have run about shouting "EUREKA!" I am not going to shout "Eureka." I am simply going to tell you to get busy now with this technique and produce its minimum, a MEST Clear. We need them. We can use a couple thousand by fall. This one really has found it. So all I am going to say is, "You've got it now! Let's get this show on the road." That isn't Greek. It's a call to action.

L. Ron Hubbard
June 1952

*Lectures available as *The Route to Infinity.*

INTRODUCTION

*T*HIS IS a cold-blooded and factual account of your last 76 trillion years.

The test of any knowledge is its usefulness. Does it make one happier or more able? By it and with it, can he better achieve his goals?

This is useful knowledge. With it the blind again see, the lame walk, the ill recover, the insane become sane and the sane become saner. By its use the thousand abilities Man has sought to recover become his once more.

Like all useful knowledge it was hardly won. I began search into the back track of Mankind some years ago. There was no actual knowledge of it in existence. There were numberless superstitions, countless guesses, as many theories in favor of one thing as in favor of another. People believed, some of them, that Man had lived before. They had no proof. Others believed that Man was born innocent and died and went to a place called Hell. Most believed that when you had lived once, that was all, fellow.

Such a number of conflicting theories must have truth in them. It became my business to discover, against considerable odds, that truth.

In the first place, there was something wrong with Man. An animal such as a cat, even a reptile, a lizard, had habit patterns which carried him through his early days. Not Man. Why not? As usual, a lot of vagueness answered this. The very schools of "thought" that said Man was "just another animal" bogged utterly on why it was that babies, the young of this very intelligent animal, are much more stupid than kittens. That was only one thing wrong with Man that wasn't explained.

The further one investigated, the more one came to understand that here, in this creature Homo sapiens, were entirely too many unknowns. People who suddenly, out of no observable training, begin to speak foreign tongues, men who "seem to remember having been here before," strange yearnings in people for various parts of the country or the world or the stars of which they have no actual knowledge—such things are routine puzzles.

And there was a much more important thing at work than mere curiosity. Now and then, in my auditing, I would discover a case which would be extremely reluctant to recover and then would recover only partially so long as I used data from the current lifetime of the preclear. But as soon as I used the whole span of the time track—about 76 trillion years—I could obtain immediate response.

One must be very impartial, even brutal, in investigation. The last series of cases I audited—twenty in number, chosen at random from various life strata and suffering from mental and physical ills which were extremely varied—were audited to demonstrate finally to myself one thing only: Can an auditor obtain a swift recovery by auditing the current lifetime only? I used the most modern of techniques—1952—and did a standard auditing address to the current lifetime of each one. I obtained mediocre results, partial recoveries, slight betterment in attitude. Then I audited each case addressing only past track, prior to this lifetime. The results were swift and spectacular. Thus I validated, for myself, the reality that in auditing the whole track, one can obtain excellent results; that in auditing the current lifetime, one can obtain slow and mediocre results. From this series came this conclusion:

THE AUDITOR WHO INSISTS ON AUDITING THE CURRENT LIFETIME ONLY, WHEN HE HAS THE WHOLE TRACK TECHNIQUE AVAILABLE, IS WASTING TIME AND EFFORT AND IS, IN FACT, SWINDLING HIS PRECLEAR.

I announced "whole track" techniques to a large number of auditors. I found the better auditors quite willing to use them and these immediately began to obtain miracle-level results. A very few held back, were very cautious, would not employ the whole track, clung to this lifetime, invalidated the E-Meter, invalidated what they erroneously called "past lives," were scathingly critical of my employing such data. So I investigated the auditors.

Several of these were given sessions by me. I found several noteworthy similarities about them. They were so low in tone it was almost impossible to get them to register on an old-style Mathison. Their cases were utterly bogged. They generally made a practice of refusing any auditing. Their general record with preclears was very poor. Their own lives were running badly. They not only fought "past lives," as they called whole track, but they fought any technique evolved since the summer of 1950 or used later techniques poorly. They would not run any "overt acts," even in this lifetime. They needed, so far as their cases were concerned, the most careful auditing. I found two people, not auditors, who objected violently to "past lives" and who were "wide-open" cases. Both were in the inaccessible band, both had unsavory social records, both protested being audited in any incident of any kind. I concluded, therefore, that the relatively sane are capable of accepting evidence and the insane are not.

Occasionally people have told me that I should not release the data contained in this volume because there would be a repercussion throughout the country which would ruin Dianetics forever. Oddly enough, I've been unable to discover this repercussion. I have found people alert and friendly toward this data. Whole track is evidently much more acceptable than the idea of a prenatal. And, witness a recent *Reader's Digest*, even the medical profession is accepting prenatals.

Further, it is very hard to argue with a miracle. Today, Eleanor has arthritis. She is audited whole track with 1952 techniques. Tonight, she doesn't have arthritis. Miracles using whole track are plentiful. By using this data, an auditor can obtain a MEST Clear rather easily.

But the best argument which can be advanced for whole track is that it is factual. By using this knowledge, more is obtained than auditing results. A preclear suddenly recovers the ability, carefully learned eighty years ago, to play a piano; an electronics engineer, doing poorly before, suddenly wraps up formulas that would puzzle Einstein and which may get Man off Earth; and a thousand details in a hundred sciences become clear.

The search of this track began some years ago and was conducted sporadically on many preclears. Various instruments such as the electroencephalograph and the police lie detector were used to further this search, but these were inadequate and limited for my purposes. Finally, Volney Mathison applied his electronic genius to the problem and invented the Electropsychometer. This instrument had a range and ability greatly in excess of anything before known. It compares to itself only in the field of physioelectrical mensuration and to existing devices as the electronic microscope compares to looking through a quartz stone. As soon as this instrument was turned loose on the problem, the problem ceased to exist. By adding up and checking probabilities on scores of persons, the character, extent and content of the whole track were mapped.

Once the E-Meter gave reliable data, the main problem became the estimation of intentions, of sources, of the reasons behind the reasons. Most of this work has been done.

It comments poorly on Man's dullness that this project was impeded and slowed greatly by lack of funds and by very active efforts on the part of some to acquire and own the copyrights of Dianetics—may the ill of the world forgive them. Thus the map is not as complete in this issue as it might be.

This work is honest research, done with considerable care. And it will bear up under survey by any competent auditor or investigator.

The most amusing aspect of the whole track is that this work bears up under the onslaught of police lie detector experts. These, hard-eyed and uncompromising, become startled half out of their wits to discover that some of the crimes they find on their machines were committed two or three "lives" ago by the criminal under test and that, most alarmingly, the crimes so discovered are discoverable again to the last detail in the police archives. This is very upsetting to these operators—to be informed so bluntly that Man lives many years, not threescore and ten, and that today's lifer may again be on their hands tomorrow as a juvenile delinquent!

Gravestones, ancient vital statistics, old diplomas and medals will verify in every detail the validity of "many lifetimes." Your E-Meter will tell you.

HOW AND WHAT

"There are two general problems in processing preclears. The first is How to audit, the second is What to audit."

TO AUDIT

Chapter One

HOW AND
WHAT TO AUDIT

HERE ARE TWO general problems in processing preclears. The first is HOW to audit, the second is WHAT to audit.

The present volume presupposes that the skill necessary to the first problem has been mastered. And there is good reason why this should be the case, for the present techniques of Dianetics are far from difficult—Technique 80, to all intents and purposes, putting the finishing touches on the knowledge necessary to handle thought.

A study of HOW to audit embraces thought, emotion and effort, counter-thought, counter-emotion and counter-effort, the three actions of energy, the behavior of attention units, the anatomy of "maybe" and a general knowledge of the background of Dianetics. Elementary group courses exist which, coupled with book study and, if possible, study with a College associate, give one all the insight and skill necessary to accomplish results.

WHAT to audit is covered, in some degree, in other literature such as *Science of Survival* and the first volume of Dianetics, *Dianetics: The Modern Science of Mental Health*, as well as *Advanced Procedure and Axioms*. The current work is, however, the first coverage of all general categories. It is written to be used in connection with *Electropsychometric Auditing* and the *Individual Track Map*—companion pieces of this present volume.

There are four general fields of incidents, four areas of past, embraced in this work. These are:

1. Present life, from preconception to present time.

2. The genetic line, being the evolutionary chain on Earth.

3. Large, specialized segments of the whole track.

4. The theta body line, or whole track.

Of the four, only the last is actually capable of producing the Clear with any rapidity. However, the auditor should be familiar with all these lines. They are taken, one by one, in the above order in this volume.

All incidents in this volume should be detected and audited with the assistance of an E-Meter. If it were not for the E-Meter, these incidents would have remained undetected except in the haziest state. Without an E-Meter, they cannot be audited with security or even safety for the preclear.

HOW to audit and WHAT to audit, together, deserve considerable study. Certainly they deserve more study than one would give American history or English or arithmetic, for they deliver a greater dividend to the individual.

Studying these incidents may be discovered to be restimulative to the student. If so, he would find auditing them as restimulative. However, such restimulation is very easily resolved and unless he feels close to the end of tolerance, he should not be shy of auditing or studying the track.

CASES:
TARGETS OF

*"The theta being is the 'I',
it is Who the preclear is."*

ADDRESS

Chapter Two

CASES: TARGETS OF ADDRESS

SEVERAL TARGETS present themselves in a case and any one of them can be audited with some profit.

The complexity of the problem of human behavior was a complexity of factors, not an unresolvable mass of twine. Once these factors are each one known and identified, very little trouble is experienced.

Thought, emotion, effort, counter-thought, counter-emotion, counter-effort, motivator attention units, overt attention units, DED attention units and their manifestation on the various Tone Scale charts are the sum and total of factors to be audited out of any one target.

Each and every auditing target contains these factors, is audited in the same way, has the same basic behavior pattern and succumbs to such auditing. It does not matter what target one is addressing in a case, he will not discover wild or unexplained manifestations in HOW he audits that target. Each one, in short, is made up of the same woof and warp. Each one is basically theta. Theta behaves and manifests in a constant manner, no matter what form it takes. Thus the auditor should quiet any apprehension he has that something he is auditing is behaving differently than a standard item.

VARIABLES, SO FAR AS HAS BEEN DISCOVERED, DO NOT EXIST IN THETA SINCE THE DISCOVERIES OF DIANETICS.

There are several targets for the auditor. If he understands thoroughly what they are, his chances of mistaking one kind of incident for another are much reduced. They are in their order of magnitude, not their importance:

Cellular Injuries

CELLULAR INJURIES comprise the first target.

A cell is a living animal all by itself. The most necessary auditing on cellular injuries is the emergency assist wherein the auditor repairs an accident, a burn, an incident which has just occurred. The auditor will find that in auditing a cellular injury which has just occurred, the somatics are very sharp and far more painful than when auditing a standard facsimile. Cellular injuries are audited no differently than any other kind of incident. However, it must be remarked that individual cells have "past lives," the easiest manifestation of past lives to check. An auditor can follow a particular cell throughout its own generations within the body and, as part of the evolutionary line, discover many injuries to it. Further, in going back on the evolutionary line and auditing an injury to a single cell, the future positions of that cell are easily located in the body from there to the present, for the future injuries blow off like small sparks of pain when the basic injury is released. The migrations of a single cell throughout the body are very easy to track in this fashion and ordinarily check against standard suppositions in the field of physical biology. The pulp of a tooth, for instance, tracks back, cell by cell, to early engrams. When these are relieved, a "toothache" in that tooth becomes almost impossible no matter how many "nerves" are exposed, a matter which brings about quite a revolution in dentistry.

Cellular injuries do not require any special kind of auditing and they comprise no special kind of injury, nor are there psychosomatics which demand that the cells alone be audited.

GENETIC ENTITY

GENETIC ENTITY, the "GE," is the second area of address.

This is the entity which carries forward from the earliest formation of the MEST body. It is this entity which has the "genetic line" engrams. It is located more or less in the center of the body, the stomach, but it is actually a composite of all the cellular experience on the line. It has the manifestation of a single identity. It was formerly referred to as the "somatic mind" (see *Dianetics: The Modern Science of Mental Health*). Out of all the past experience of the MEST body, it makes up a form—a working carbon-oxygen engine. It has no real personality. It is not the "I" of the body. It has a record, in many cases, of the entire experience forward until the last life. The GE has the record of past deaths. Auditing it alters physical structure, eradicates physical malformations. But these can be otherwise changed—by auditing the theta being. The GE facsimiles include a transfer of somatics from past theta beings, for it is not common for a GE to have the same theta being twice. The GE is the constant and continual workhorse of the theta body. It regulates the heartbeat, takes care of all such responses, acts as a stimulus-response mind to avoid pain and discover pleasure, and keeps the body running in general. A GE departs from the body much later than the theta beings abandon one, sees it through the death to the end and only then leaves to join the line once more some two or three days before conception.

This is the "mind" of an animal, a dog or a cat or a cow.

INJECTED ENTITIES

INJECTED ENTITIES are the third class of target.

These are actually synthetics. They are ridges that think. They form a very complex pattern. They have geographical areas in the body. These areas are standard, preclear to preclear. These areas answer up on an E-Meter like actual minds rather than compartments of a mind.

The areas are: the CENTER (forehead and down); the RIGHT INSIDE (from the edge of the jaw halfway out to the shoulder); the RIGHT OUTSIDE (from halfway to the shoulder to the point of the shoulder); the LEFT INSIDE (opposite from the right inside); the LEFT OUTSIDE (opposite from the right outside); the STOMACH ENTITY (located in the area of the solar plexus); plus various other entities held in by these basic entities.

These entities run off their own past deaths on other tracks, hold sections of the body paralyzed, bar areas from being audited, withhold information from "I" and do other mischief. They are actually the basis of "demon circuits" (as covered in *Dianetics: The Modern Science of Mental Health*) and they mirror the personality of persons antipathetic to the preclear. They are entirely stimulus-response. Each one has, from preclear to preclear, the same personality in the same body position. The right inside, for instance, answers up to the name of "crew chief." They are male and female. Their source is probably a "softened-up" theta being and they disappear when electronic incidents are audited. Prior to their disappearance, they can exhibit a wonderful and awesome role in confusing the preclear. The auditor can move the attention of the preclear into one of these and audit it through a death or painful experience and so bring it up to present time. In view of the fact that auditing basic electronic incidents eradicates them, little attention need be paid to them by the auditor beyond knowing that they are there, that they are the "mysterious voices" in the heads of some preclears, that they make critical or commanding remarks to him and serve, in general, as a fine source of aberration. Paralysis, anxiety stomachs, arthritis and many ills and aberrations have been relieved by auditing them. An E-Meter shows them up and makes them confess their misdeeds. They are probably just compartments of the mind which, cut off, begin to act as though they were persons.

Here is an inexhaustible source of study and speculation which I leave to another, having located the method of wiping them out without paying any attention to them.

THETA BEINGS

THETA BEINGS are the fourth and only really important target for the auditor.

The theta being is the "I", it is WHO the preclear is. If all the entities and beingnesses of the preclear were hydrogen balloons locked up inside him and each had a name and identity, the auditor might be confused (and the preclear *is* confused) as to who "I" is. But if the preclear were suddenly opened and the balloons let loose, the "I" balloon would float free, clear and unmistakable. And that "I" balloon would be the theta being. It would be who the preclear always thought he was anyway. All others are simply modifiers. The theta being does not get lost. It does not go away, it cannot be stolen. If it went away, the preclear would be with it and be it. The vagueness of personal identity is caused by the confusion of the theta being, not its "inextricable" tanglement with other identities.

The theta being can be confused in itself, it can be hypnotized, it can go to sleep. It can experience emotions. It can think. It can feel pain. It is immortal in that it cannot die—but it could possibly become so burdened with facsimiles that it could not continue along with bodies. It does not need a body to think, make facsimiles, experience emotions, remember or perceive.

The theta being seems natively capable of producing considerable MEST energy. Facsimiles alone inhibit this ability. Whereas it has come to feel, in association with the bad company of genetic entities and the MEST universe, that it is a stimulus-response thing, it is quite capable of generating thought independently of previous effort, counter-effort or experience.

The preclear is not guarding or harboring or hiding his theta being—he *is* his theta being. A relaxed understanding of this will prevent a considerable confusion on the part of the auditor and preclear. If the preclear is responding rationally, he is the theta being responding.

As the theta being can be "put to sleep," it is possible to bring then to the surface a GE or another entity which, using the motor controls of the body, can talk or experience. But the individual himself is not usually aware of what happened then. The various strange multipersonality manifestations of the mind are occasioned by valences and their basics, the entities. Ordinarily, unless the preclear is obviously insane, these sub-personalities are not distinctly units in themselves, but only color the activities of the theta being.

Hypnotism is the process of bringing into being the GE or other entity by putting the theta being into unconsciousness.

Self-hypnosis is the process of the theta being hypnotizing the GE or other entity and setting up a compulsive or inhibitive circuit with it.

The auditor must know that the existence of a MEST body within the fields of the theta being is incidental and even unfortunate for processing, which in the absence of a body goes much faster.

The theta being is both outside and inside the MEST body. It is not just inside. The only reason it is inside at all is that any field would penetrate the MEST body. The MEST body should not be thought of as a harbor or vessel for the theta being. A better example would be a sliver inserted unwantedly in the thumb, where the thumb would be the theta being, the MEST body the sliver. MEST bodies are good identification tags, they generate exciting emotions, they are fun to operate at times, but they are no end of existence.

A theta being, with its alertness restored, is capable of remolding the human body within its field, taking off weight here, restoring it there, changing appearance and even height. The body can also be altered by auditing cells or the GE. All in all, bodies are very easy to handle where their condition is concerned. The question is, rather: Are they practical? The theta being can evidently manufacture bodies or a reasonable facsimile thereof which, while they do not labor, neither do they have to be fed.

To a society quite mad on the subject of MEST bodies, very aberrated on "care of the body," the foregoing may seem a trifle strange and one might think the writer had, to be short, slipped a cable or two in his wits. Indeed, it is very probable that critics may say so, for their reality is entirely outraged by such sudden statements.

But this matter has been under investigation for a year and a half, as witness Theta Clear on the *Science of Survival* Tone Scale chart which I drew in January 1951. It states that the capabilities of a Theta Clear were "unknown." Now they are not so unknown and while there is much to learn about them still, much can be stated concerning them as clear fact. Back of these statements is a two-year public record of making statements which, under grueling investigation by others, turn out to be exactly what they were said to be.

Before turning away from the above, try Technique 88 and learn again what it is to be truly FREE. An hour's auditing will prove it.

THE

PRESENT

"The present life is important
out of proportion to the small
fraction of total age of
the theta being."

T h r e e

LIFE

Chapter Three

THE
PRESENT LIFE

THE PRESENT LIFE is always of considerable interest to the preclear.

In the first place, he is continuing to live in the environment and society, usually, in which he is being audited. He must still face situations which the auditor will discover. The dramatis personae of this period are, to some extent, still living or their artifacts are yet in plain view.

In the second place, the preclear is still connected to these incidents by the identifying label of his present life name and he is continually called by this label and has it confused with himself.

In the third place, these facsimiles have not been invalidated by the shock of a death and the "helpful hands" of the "between-lives" crew and so are normally visible.

Fourthly, in this life we have the combination of the current genetic being and the current theta being and their struggle to even the harsh roadway of living and their divergence of goals.

Present life, or any life that comes to view, should be to some extent cleared up for the preclear. This is very swiftly done with Symbological Processing, a volume of recent issue for use in counseling, or with an application of Technique 80 to this life or any life.

Lives are, to some extent, units in themselves. This is caused by the fact that each life, while the preclear has been "with body," is lived with a different basic team:

The GENETIC BEING carries on through the evolutionary line, parallel with the protoplasmic line, generation to generation, usually on the same planet—in this case, Earth.

The THETA BEING comes into the line from various quarters and each time usually enters an entirely different GE line. Any one life, then, is lived with a different GE.

The PRECLEAR is always and always was and always will be the theta being. But the theta being has, life to life, a different GE. The character and quality of the MEST body, then, is different in each lifetime. The past of the MEST body in each lifetime is different from the viewpoint of the theta being. Thus the theta being has variation of experience which is not always, life to life, the same pattern. Thus when lives come to view, they should be explored and audited as above. A few hours spent in this can materially assist a recovery.

The present life is important out of proportion to the small fraction of total age of the theta being. The auditor will find himself, in most cases, compelled to spend many hours upon it. But he should not audit any heavy incidents in the present lifetime. These have basics which reduce much more swiftly and these basics are always earlier by many ages. The time spent on the present life earlier in Dianetics was very great. It required scores or hundreds of hours of auditing to achieve optimum results. And then, only with great cunning could the auditor achieve his goal. Swifter techniques made present life much easier to audit, cut down the time required and increased the results. But the same results can be achieved much more swiftly, with much less skill and cunning, when one audits whole track—meaning, the track of the theta being.

Just as "medical science" has accepted prenatal experience (according to their best heralds, the popular magazines such as *Coronet* and *Reader's Digest*), prenatals fade into the obscurity of curiosa in Dianetics.

28

Great as the results were which occurred when one audited prenatals, results in the same time are now so incomparably greater in auditing the whole track, or even in using Technique 80, that one need know very little about prenatals. In the first place, it has been discovered that prenatals happen to the GE, not the theta being. These recordings are so phonograph-record-like because they are wholly in the somatic mind (the GE). They deeply affect the current MEST body structure in many ways, but this structure can be otherwise repaired.

The genetic entity apparently enters the protoplasm line some two days or a week prior to conception. There is some evidence that the GE is actually double, one entering on the sperm side, one entering on the ovum side. If the matter were still important, some time could be spent determining this, for the GE answers dually in present time.

The GE continues as the guiding genius throughout prenatal life, building, regulating the heartbeat and attending to complex structural matters. It records every perception present, asleep or awake, conscious or unconscious (in knockout or drugged sense), to the number of the (about) fifty perceptions present. Just as the doctor quite often hears a baby in a womb cry, just as he can hear its heartbeat with his stethoscope, so can the child hear what is occurring outside the mother. This is a very important datum from the standpoint of Preventive Dianetics, for by knowing it one can easily forecast the health and mental poise of a child after birth by making certain that it has a good prenatal existence. Psychotics often dramatize (re-enact) these prenatal engrams and a trip through a sanitarium will show an auditor many prenatals in full play, running off like records, ending and starting again endlessly. (You get these people out of such dramatization by using Technique 80 with symbols as in Symbological Processing or by directly auditing the "overt acts" they have done against the family or, if the dramatization is the overt act in full play, auditing the "motivator" which is occasionally a prenatal.)

Here is the list of prenatals. They can be any combination of action known to the business of living, but these are the common ones:

PRENATAL INCIDENTS

All incidents in any environment are prone to be repeated. Thus these incidents commonly appear in long chains, many incidents in each, each incident much the same as the last. To audit the chain, one should get the basic on that chain:

COITUS CHAIN, father

COITUS CHAIN, lover

CONSTIPATION CHAIN

ORDINARY BOWEL CHAIN

DOUCHE CHAIN

SICKNESS CHAIN, mother's illness

SICKNESS CHAIN, another member of the family's illness

WORK CHAIN, mother's heavy activities at work

EXERCISE CHAIN, mother's activity in sports or calisthenics

MORNING SICKNESS CHAIN

CONTRACEPTIVE CHAIN

FIGHT CHAIN, family quarrels

FIGHT CHAIN, outside the home

HIGH BLOOD PRESSURE CHAIN, mother's high blood pressure

DOCTOR EXAMINATION CHAIN, punching mother

ALCOHOL CHAIN, mother's drinking

ACCIDENT CHAIN, mother's falls and bumps

ATTEMPTED ABORTION, SURGICAL

ATTEMPTED ABORTION, DOUCHE

ATTEMPTED ABORTION BY PRESSURE

ATTEMPTED ABORTION BY EXERCISE OR JUMPING

COUGH CHAIN, mother's coughing

COUGH CHAIN, other members of family

HICCUP CHAIN

MASTURBATION CHAIN, mother's masturbation

CRYING CHAIN, mother's crying

Pre-sperm recordings are quite ordinary. The sperm sequence itself is worthy of note, for it is a race of which the sperm is very conscious. His travails in reaching the ovum are many. There is a "visio," which is quite standard, of the race. There is quite often a light, a spark, in this sequence. The sperm reaches the ovum and merges. This merging is another incident—conception.

Pre-ovum sequences are on record, but are not common. The rolling of the ovum down the tube is commonly recorded.

Conception and the impulses generated answer the conditions for one type of cancer—embryonic.

Mitosis is an incident. Cellular division, once or many times, is on common record. Mitosis answers the conditions for the other type of cancer—malignant cell.

Cancer has reportedly been eradicated by auditing out conception and mitosis.

The theta being apparently joins the track immediately prior to birth. Its sequence for itself is DEATH, BETWEEN-LIVES, BIRTH, all in a few minutes according to some findings, a sequence which is quite aberrative.

The theta being's joining is called the STARTER. The theta being sometimes fights away another theta being, sometimes considers this an overt act.

You may audit an entire prenatal bank without getting as much rise in the preclear's tone as auditing one Starter. For the theta being, after all, is the preclear.

BIRTH is a very aberrative affair and a difficult or complicated birth can aberrate the entire lifetime of the MEST body. But this means that birth should be without conversation, in a darkened and quiet room with high humidity and without drafts, not that you should audit births. In other words, one should know how aberrative birth is, but one should not audit birth as a practice. One "Facsimile One" has as many as eighty thousand births on it as locks. Birth presents itself to be audited much of the time because mother, by complaining of how difficult the preclear's birth was, makes it into an overt act. This overt act had birth as a motivator. Thus preclears are anxious to have their birth engram audited.

INFANT and CHILDHOOD ILLNESSES are important because in them the theta being loses much of the control of the body. The incidents of degradation which precede these, however, are a more important target for the auditor.

Most preclears are stuck somewhere on the present life track. The E-Meter will tell the auditor where if the auditor asks in terms of years. It is rarely where the preclear thinks it is. Operations, accidents, illnesses are all, more or less, routine. The auditor should take them as he is given them by the E-Meter or symbols or both. But he should not audit them as such unless he is strongly forced to do so—the incidents on which they depend are so much earlier, so much more aberrative.

For every motivator in the present life, there is an overt or a DED. Thus it behooves the auditor to pay much more attention to using Technique 80 than it does to find new and strange present life incidents to audit.

IT SHOULD NOT REQUIRE MORE THAN A SCORE OF HOURS TO CLEAN UP THE PRESENT LIFE UNTIL HEAVY INCIDENTS IN THE PAST CAN BE AUDITED.

(This is true for the neurotic and relatively sane only. It is not true for psychotics. For them, it may be necessary to audit prenatals or use other techniques and to spend perhaps hundreds of hours of ARC Processing to make them entirely sane and stable.)

Present life incidents, by test, cannot quickly resolve any case. Audit present life only until one can audit theta-line material with safety.

THE

GENETIC

"One can discover when
the theta being first came
to Earth..."

LINE

Chapter Four

THE GENETIC LINE

HE GENETIC LINE consists of the total of incidents which have occurred during the evolution of the MEST body itself. The composite of these facsimiles has the semblance of a being. This being would be called the GENETIC ENTITY or the GE.

The GE is not an actual individual, but a composite of individualities assumed in the single lives along the evolutionary track.

The discovery of the GE makes it possible at last to vindicate the theory of evolution proposed by Darwin and to discover the various missing connections in the line as well as to explore the characteristics, goals and developmental urges of organisms on the evolutionary line.

Further, the discovery of the GE makes it possible to adjust hitherto contrary material in the theory of evolution.

Darwin and others proposed some scores of years since that an animal body was developed by necessity into successive organisms, each one better adjusted to its environment. The organisms began in simplicity and graduated through successive eons into complexity.

37

Darwin proposed that natural selection was the guiding principle and that protoplasm, genes, etc., were alone capable of modifying the organism. Later workers proposed ingenious theories of electronic mutation.

Prior to these discoveries of Darwin and others, Earthmen accepted various impossibilities as the explanation of the variety of animal forms. The Vedic theories persisted until the early A.D.'s when a new cult arose in the Middle East (30° N. Lat., 30° to 80° E. Long., Earth) and proposed that animals had been created suddenly from mud by a Creator and that this included Man. The Vedic peoples had proposed much earlier that a sort of evolution was responsible for the various forms.

Darwin and his co-workers picked up this theory after the Vedic Hymns had been transplanted to Europe, about a century earlier, concurrent with the French-English conquest of India. Considerable turmoil resulted from the introduction of the Darwinian theories as these were then in direct contrast with the existing superstition. A trial of a schoolteacher, who dared teach the theory of evolution in a backwoods area of the United States, resulted in a victory for the superstition—the schoolteacher standing convicted. But evolution received so much publicity over the world, as a result, that it is now the generally taught theory in schools.

However, one should not think of evolution as a standard or precise theory. It is a sprawling and contradictory mass of poorly compiled data, taken from ancient swamps and tar pits, and there are many schools of evolution. These are taught un-uniformly in biology classes. Biology is based on "cytology," or the study of cells. Existing theory in cytology is quite contradictory to various tenets of evolution. In other words, the field is poorly integrated and badly understood and not overly gifted with data.

The discoveries in Scientology can be addressed to these sciences of biology and cytology with considerable profit. By auditing previously uninformed preclears up this evolutionary line, the results are similar if not identical.

The most direct address to altering the shape and form of the MEST body of the preclear is the auditing of the evolutionary line. Many illnesses, aches and pains are residual in the body line itself. These are restimulated by the environment or the thoughts and actions of the theta being and, once restimulated, alter the physical condition of the body. However, the body is responsive in present time to the command of a restrengthened theta being and the shape and condition of the body can be otherwise changed than by solely addressing the GE.

Single or multiple cells respond, each one, as though it had its own GE. Very early on the time track, in the area of the "Photon Converter" or the "Helper," the GE and the cell entity are the same, for here the incidents are single-cell incidents.

The theory of the EPICENTERS applies very particularly along the MEST evolutionary line. This theory holds that in any given generation on the evolutionary line, the sum of its counter-efforts will form, in the next generation, the new command post. Every central relay point of the nerve system has been, at some time or another on the evolutionary line, a command post or a sub-command post of the organism. As the organism develops these command posts, each one is subjected to new counter-efforts which form the area of the new command post. Thus the body has many old command posts from which the "somatic mind" (or GE) controlled all the responses of the body. The "funny bone" in the elbow is an old sub-command post, an old epicenter. Any point of reflex response in the body was an old command post or sub-command post. These epicenters stand along the nerve channels of the body and are like switchboards. They still command their immediate areas and, independently of the central command post in the brain, can cause reaction in their area.

The best example of this, and the most important point for the auditor, is the fact that two separate lines once merged (mollusk) and thereafter worked together as a team. These lines, each one, now has its own command post, its own memory bank.

These two lines are the right and left brain lobes. The one in ascendancy ordinarily commands the one in subjugation. The right side of the brain controls the left side of the body. The left side of the brain controls the right side of the body. Malcoordination of the two halves of the body can be traced to imbalance or confusion or outright warfare between these two control centers. Half-paralysis, stroke, anesthetized areas can be traced in part to this malcoordination of the present lifetime epicenters. Each one of these goes back as itself along the same track, generation to generation, sharing the same experiences, until one reaches the mollusk or bivalve stage where each one has a prior and independent and separate history. Either one is capable of controlling the whole body. In the bivalve state, one finds them at war with each other in an effort to attain sole command of the entire bivalve.

Right- and left-handedness are caused by these malcoordinations of the two lines. Actually, one should be neither right-handed nor left-handed, but ambidextrous. An entire technique, complete within itself, was worked out some months ago when I first encountered these phenomena. This technique has been working so well for some auditors that they wonder why any newer data is introduced. The technique consists of obtaining optimum communication amongst all epicenters in the body with the result of a complete unity of action by the body. This does a great deal for timing and coordination in general and has been known to eradicate severe psychosomatic ills. Theta-line techniques, being addressed to "I" rather than to the MEST body, produce swifter results.

Here is a wealth of material for the investigator. The principal incidents and circumstances on this line have already been located and were located before this data was released the first time. But innumerable structural puzzles are resolved with this data and few are the preclears whose bodies do not react vigorously to the suggestion that some of these incidents may exist, so violent is the charge contained in these incidents. An E-Meter has been known to drop as much as twenty dials on the auditor's faint hint of the existence of the "Helper" or the "Weeper."

Life on the evolutionary line is grim, very tooth and claw. So overpoweringly awesome has been life on this line that the violence pervaded the social theory of psychology for decades and, indeed, has underlain the most basic philosophies of Man's behavior. Here, at the very least, is the explanation for so many theories in the past.

It should not be overlooked that on this GE line one finds what the uninitiated call "past lives." This continuous living on the part of the somatic mind does not end with the ape. It continues right on through to present time. The GE contains enormous amounts of data about recent times and past times.

The GE in America seems to have followed the track of the Western civilizations. This accounts in part for the strange fact that our histories give us enormous treatises on Greece and nothing on Persia, great tomes on Rome and little on Egypt, enormous writings on that small continent Europe and very little on Asia. A correct track of civilization is not from Phoenicia, through Greece, Rome and Europe to America. It is from China through Chaldea, through Babylonia, through Persia, through Achaea and minorly through Greece, Rome and Europe, since these last form a decline from statures much greater than they before them. The American GE enters civilizations at various times and periods. It usually passed through Greece and Rome and Europe, which accounts for our fixation on these minor empires and inferior societies.

The point here is that a study of history is very restimulative to the GE and produces body alterations for which the theta being, not having been there usually, cannot account.

YOU, as a theta being, may or may not have seen Greece or Rome.

Your MEST GE has probably activated a body there, just as it has been (in accordance with Darwin and his Russian copyist, one of the patron saints of the twentieth century slave state of Russia, Lysenko) an anthropoid in the deep forests of forgotten continents or a mollusk seeking to survive on the shores of some lost sea.

By the way, if you cannot take a warning, your discussion of these incidents with the uninitiated in Scientology can produce havoc. Should you describe the "Clam" to someone, you may restimulate it in him to the extent of causing severe jaw hinge pain. One such victim, after hearing about a clam death, could not use his jaws for three days. Another "had to have" two molars extracted because of the resulting ache. The "Clam" and all these incidents are very much present in the GE and can be restimulated easily.

So do not be sadistic with your describing them to people—unless, of course, they belligerently claim that Man has no past memory for his evolution. In that event, describe away. It makes believers over and above enriching your friend the dentist who, indeed, could not exist without these errors and incidents on the evolutionary line!

The auditor should know about this line, for it sometimes crosses the theta line—which is to say, it is "co-experienced" in places by the theta being. This is simple to unravel. Also, the preclear may have a GE incident in such forceful restimulation that the auditor has no choice but to audit it. When one says "GE incident," he means of course anything on the entire evolutionary line including "past lives."

One must not forget that the theta being has also shared, with another (not the present) GE, some of these past life experiences. One can discover when the theta being first came to Earth, when it first had a MEST body on Earth and so discover its first contact with some MEST body line. It has co-experienced with a GE in every life where it has had a MEST body.

There are extraterrestrial GEs, perhaps, GEs which evolved elsewhere and which are still elsewhere. These GEs would be on the evolutionary line of some other planet. They would not cross into this evolutionary line. But the theta being, where it has had a MEST body on some other planet, may have had it in company with a GE there which had its own peculiarities. One almost never audits such a thing, but it is remarked that it can be there.

The following incidents are audited with the usual tools of Dianetics and Scientology, with due attention to Technique 80. One may wonder what a clam might consider an overt act. The best way to find out is to put it on the E-Meter and ask. Every one of these, when in evidence to be audited, is part of a motivator–overt combination. When they do not react on a meter, when they do not present themselves to be audited, don't bother to go looking for them. If they are to be audited, they will react with violence—as much as a five- or twenty-dial drop on an E-Meter. If they drop in such a fashion, there is a companion incident—which is to say that they have motivators where they are overt acts and overt acts where they are motivators. Such a drop means that they are being used in present time as motivators or overt acts.

THE ATOM

Lucretius said that each ATOM was life. This may or may not be true. But the first incident one finds in the GE behaves as though the preclear were an atom, complete with electronic rings. This incident audits very poorly until it is located as a companion to some overt act.

There seems to be a "hole in space" immediately ahead of the Atom. Just after this hole is a condition of motion, with the preclear in the center, with rings of motion traveling around him.

Characteristic of this incident is a state of mind wanting no ARC, neither to receive ARC nor to give ARC, wanting *no* ARC give or take. This is a comfortable aloneness. The preclear usually perceives from this his later necessities for ARC on a MEST level.

THE COSMIC IMPACT

As physicists tell us, COSMIC RAYS enter the body in large numbers and occasionally explode in the body. Very early on the track, the impact of a Cosmic Ray and its explosion is very destructive to the existing organism.

One is "accepting" rays and suddenly one explodes. Sometimes one is accepting one while another explodes elsewhere. This has been found fairly basic on an anxiety stomach, on acceptance–rejection confusions.

Remember that in all early incidents, there is a GE line for the left side of the body and one for the right side and either one can affect the whole body when it is run. Thus there are Atoms for the right and left and Cosmic Rays for the right and left sides both.

THE PHOTON CONVERTER

All early life is fixated on CONVERTING PHOTONS to energy. One finds the algae and the plankton taking their living from photons from the sun and minerals from the sea.

Because at night there is no sunlight, the Photon Converter sinks into an apathy which eons later becomes the MEST body's craving for sleep. This is a basic problem of no energy received, very little storage for energy.

All Photon Converter incidents are concerned with light and dark, the storms of the sea, the fight to keep from rolling into the surf. The fear of and combat with the merciless surf is characteristic of all early incidents until well after the "Weeper." Sending the ill to the seashore to listen to surf is a guaranteed restimulator.

There are many types of these incidents. A basic one is concerned with fear of sinking, effort to rise, for the Photon Converter must stay afloat.

Past deaths as a Photon Converter are common. For only by dying and knowing how one died could the GE utilize the chief counter-efforts which menaced. A chain of experience which did not include death would not be able to build efficient organisms and would be unprofitable. Death on the GE line has a very great value and marks progress. Death on the theta line is so much wasted time. Hence, the quarrel between the GE and the theta being.

44

THE HELPER

The HELPER is one of the most powerful incidents in terms of charge on the early track. It is actually mitosis, or cell splitting.

The GE carries along, a tiny cell, mobile and swimming. Suddenly it decides to divide. It starts to split in half. There is usually an enormous struggle in this splitting. One side wants to split, the other usually does not want to split. Having split, one side is energetic and starts to go about its business. Then it sees that the other side is limp and falling toward the mud below the water. The energetic side turns and dives and tries to nudge the other up to the surface, tries to revive it. The failing side may revive. In the incidents you will find, there will be one of two outcomes: the failing side fails despite the other's efforts; the failing side revives and now, all energetic, swims away, leaving to his fate the other that helped it and who is now too weak to live and so sinks and dies.

There are two sides to the Helper: The whole sequence of the losing side is present; the whole sequence of the winning side is present. The confusion lies in the fact that each is itself, but a moment ago was the other. There are whole squads of Helpers. It is a confusing area for the GE which therein has much cause for misidentification.

THE CLAM

A variety of incidents may intervene between the HELPER and the WEEPER. These are the evolution chain which includes jellyfish, seaweed and some other forms.

It is interesting that immobile states are most liable to have heavy incidents. It is also interesting that bulbous seaweed, uprooted and cast ashore by storms, gave Man some of his early experiences with sunlight in the absence of water. A distinct somatic of drying and itching is felt by preclears when they encounter this incident, a restimulation of the drying outer skin of the dying seaweed.

It is also interesting that bulbous seaweed is an early pattern of Man's later general form. Jellyfish incidents are quite remarkable for their occasional aberrative force. The jellyfish sometimes drifts into a cave or grotto and is pressed against the stone by rising tide and waves, thus gaining the first facsimiles which later become a shell as in the clam. Here is an example of the principle of counter-efforts molding the physical shape and necessities of life forms.

The CLAM is a deadly incident, but mostly when restimulated on purpose. Although this area of the track is called the Clam, it is improbable that the actual animal was a clam such as our razorbacks. Visios on this seem to indicate that it is a scalloped-lip, white-shelled creature. The Clam was, of course, quite thoroughly fixed to the rocks and the state is very static. The Clam had many troubles. The first of these troubles is the double-hinge problem. One hinge wishes to stay open, the other tries to close. Thus conflict occurs. Here we have two control centers, both of them more or less equal in power, having no internal communication.

In the jellyfish, we have the first Third Dynamic engrams where the goal is to hold together at all costs. As soon as the hinges are formed in the Clam, we have our first efforts to be completely contrary and internally at war. The solution occurs when one hinge goes into apathy and the other assumes complete control.

The hinge epicenters later become the hinges of the human jaw. Should you desire to confirm this, describe to some uninitiated person the death of a clam without saying what you are describing: "Can you imagine a clam sitting on the beach, opening and closing its shell very rapidly?" (Make a motion with your thumb and forefinger of a rapid opening and closing.) The victim may grip his jaws with his hand and feel quite upset. He may even have to have a few teeth pulled. At the very least, he will argue as to whether or not the shell stays open at the end or closed. And he will, with no hint of the death aspect of it, talk about the "poor clam" and he will feel quite sad emotionally.

The Clam had an astonishing number of adventures for so minor a creature. It would get things into its shell and be unable to get them out. It would get its shell stuck open and be unable to shut it. And it would come loose from its rocks under the surface of the water and get tossed into the broil of the surf. And it would become deserted by the tide and left to bake under a frying sun, a quite uncomfortable situation which restimulates sometimes in a sunburn.

There was or is a spore method of procreation used by the Clam. The spore was put on the inside of the lip and permitted to grow. Eventually it became large enough to become a Clam on its own and would depart. There is a guardian-emotion on the part of the Clam for these spores, and a sadness on their departure. But there is more to the spore than this. The spore was like a barnacle. When the Clam was cast ashore, these spores were still alive in the shell. The sun would kill the inner cells of the "barnacle" while the outer shell cells still lived. The dead inner cells would form a gas which, under the heat, would explode violently—to the agony of the living barnacle shell cells. This bursting was sudden and painful. These spores gave incidents which permitted the human teeth to have a pattern. The ancient bursting engrams are still dramatized by the teeth which, under stress, burst or feel like bursting. Running out some of these bursting incidents will take the ache out of a tooth rapidly. The "fifth nerve channel" is around the mouth and is heavy out of all proportion. A nerve channel is as heavy as it has to be to conduit pain away from the area. Thus I deduced that there must have been much pain in this area and that the "fifth channel" is the oldest main conduit—and so it is. Audit all such incidents for all teeth and you have permanently taken the pain out of toothache and cut down decay. By the way, a barnacle, because of this bursting possibility, at length developed a "blow-out area"—a cap which would blow easily. And teeth have such an area. It gives way and makes cavities.

The Clam had many, many deaths. A scan across its deaths locates the one in restimulation. You will be amazed to find the Clam sufficiently advanced as a cellular-somatic mind to have postulates, to think thoughts.

The Clam is actually a group of incidents rather than a single one.

The Weeper

After leaving the sea, the GE spent a half a million years on the beach. It had already known about air as a plankton, had known about the beach as seaweed and dying clam. But it nevertheless required some half a million years, according to the evolutionists, for the creature to learn to use the land.

The plights of the WEEPER are many and pathetic. Still obtaining its food from the waves, it yet had to breathe. Waves are impetuous and often irregular. The Weeper would open up to get food from the water and get a wave in the shell. It would vigorously pump out the water and try to get some air and then, before it could gulp atmosphere, be hit by another wave. Here was anxiety. Being still a shell animal, the mobility of the Weeper is poor. It could not withdraw rapidly nor advance rapidly. Tides went out and left it to bake and thirst. The sand got into it. And it had to pump water swiftly in order to continue to live.

The Weeper is so called because it had to pump salt water. It was deduced that crying in a human being is very unnatural. Why is it that a human being has to pump out some salt water in order to feel better—which is to say, why does crying out a grief charge produce such a change in a case? The incident must be one of pumping out salt water. And this is practically the total activity of the Weeper which, living perilously on the edge of the surf, had to pump to eat and to breathe. The creature had two pumping tubes. These later became, because they were furthest toward the light, the eyes of the human being. These tubes had very rough treatment, getting full of sand, being battered by surf.

The inability of a preclear to cry is partly a hang-up in the Weeper. He is about to be hit by a wave, has his eyes full of sand or is frightened about opening his shell because he may be hit. An occluded case is sometimes merely a case of "shell-shut."

Get the preclear to imagine that his eyes are in his mouth, looking out. Get him to scan through such a situation. You will find the Weeper which he has in restimulation.

If you make a preclear go through all the physical motions of sobbing convulsively, no matter what his emotion may be, he may connect with the Weeper. Belching, gasping, sobbing, choking, shuddering, trembling are all manifestations of emotional dramatization of the Weeper.

The Weeper (originally called the "Grim Weeper" or the "Boohoo") had trillions of misadventures. Scanning over these, the auditor will find the one or two which have remained in restimulation and which are open to auditing.

THE VOLCANOES

Earth was undergoing VOLCANIC UPHEAVALS during the days of life on the beach. Possibly it was this volcanic action which severed the chain of evolution, for there is a lack of real reason why this evolution should not be continuing on even today. The progress of evolution was cut at the beach, possibly, because the beach is peculiarly subject to violence during volcanic upheavals—sea and land being in clash. Now and then the auditor will find a Volcanic Upheaval incident in restimulation, with its palls of choking sulfurous smoke. It has been suggested that smoking tobacco is a sort of dramatization of volcanoes which, at the least, were spectacular.

THE BIRDS

Occasionally the creatures of the beach, still shell animals, had their troubles with BIRDS which had become so earlier. Birds of a very crude construction developed a taste for clams. Clams had no adequate defense against them. If a clam opened its shell, the bird would thrust in a beak or a claw. If the clam then closed, the bird would fly up into the air. The clam would let go, drop on a rock and become bird food. If the clam didn't close, it became bird food anyway.

Falling sensations, indecision and other troubles go with the Birds.

Sometimes a preclear will come up with an incident where he was a bird or even a bat. The auditor should be very careful about what he would call dub-in. For this one belongs not in the GE, but most likely in the theta line with the preclear taking over the body or form of a bird or bat. The incident is quite valid. It does not, however, belong on the GE line.

Theta-line incidents occasionally restimulate and group with GE incidents. Auditing brings them apart easily. Thus it is in the case of the Birds. For theta beings can fly.

BEING EATEN

In that so many fish and animals were equipped with so many teeth, it is inevitable that somebody somewhere on the track would have been eaten. And so it is, for there are a great many BEING EATEN engrams. These minor circumstances are, of course, motivators. The auditor should realize that the GE itself did some eating and thus there are many of these Eating engrams which are motivators. Diet faddists, people who will not eat meat, are hung in "maybes" on the subject of digesting and being digested. Many strange psychosomatic ills and skin manifestations may be traced to these incidents.

Anyone who knows Technique 80 knows that dispersal of energy is a difficult condition to run. The GE, about to be eaten by a fish, suddenly recognizes the fact and his attention units disperse. In fact, he may disperse right off the couch. Few auditors, in the absence of Technique 80, have been able to run Being Eaten incidents. Knowing about the dispersal of attention units and knowing that this is fear may permit an auditor at last to run and reduce these Being Eaten incidents.

There is a strange compliance on the part of the GE, in some cases, to be eaten. Later on, this may take on the form of compliance in being beaten or abused. Masochism on the GE line may have its seat in such incidents.

50

There is an "emotion" of being able to at least assist the survival of another body by letting it be fed.

Auditing an Eating incident consists of requiring the preclear to locate the dispersal of his attention units and the center of that dispersal. The attention units may be located far behind the GE in the Eating incident and should be traced from there back to the preclear until they are reduced.

THE SLOTH

There are many steps and incidents between the BIRDS and the SLOTH. However, they are most of them mobile and few of them are found in high restimulation. With the Sloth, we again find the GE in a state which is not very mobile, not easily defensible, in a world where the evolutionary line has produced more developed and more carnivorous beings.

Man's line is not very pugnacious. The GE is smarter in Man's line than the GEs in other lines, but Man's current intelligence comes from an entirely different quarter than evolution. The Sloth shows Man's nature well, so far as GEs are concerned: "Leave me alone and I'll leave you alone" is the philosophy here. But the Sloth was slow and easily attacked. And he had bad times falling out of trees when hit by snakes, falling off cliffs when attacked by baboons. And the Sloth was trying to *think*. The most pitiful painful efforts at thinking are found in this series.

The Sloth is a chain of incidents and misadventures, mostly showing up fear of snakes and of falling.

THE APE

When Man had advanced as far as the APE, he was agile and intelligent.

The Ape is usually an area of overt acts against animals and incidents of protecting young.

THE PILTDOWN MAN

Man's first real Manhood is found in the PILTDOWN, a creature not an ape, yet not entirely a man. It is so named not because it is accurately the real Piltdown Man, but because it has some similarity.

The Piltdown contains freakish acts of strange "logic," of demonstrating dangerousness on one's fellows, of eating one's wife and other somewhat illogical activities. The Piltdown teeth were *enormous* and he was quite careless as to who and what he bit and often very surprised at the resulting damage.

Obsessions about biting, efforts to hide the mouth and early familial troubles can be found in the Piltdown. It is a wonderful area in which to locate GE overt acts.

THE CAVEMAN

Keeping women at home, for men, and keeping a man from keeping one at home, for women, can be found in the CAVEMAN.

Here one crippled one's woman to keep her there or poisoned one's man for having kept her there. Marital malaction often goes back to the Caveman. Any condition of interpersonal relationships can be found in this area. Jealousy and overt acts around it—strangling, smashing in heads with rocks, quarrels about homes, tribal rebukes, pack instincts—can be found in the Caveman.

PAST DEATHS

It must be kept in mind that PAST DEATHS happened to the GE and to the theta being. Any GE has a regular line of past deaths, coming on forward chronologically.

The auditor may have some difficulty locating GE deaths in the last few thousand years because deaths are also registered on the theta line. The GE under processing may have had hundreds of theta beings in command of it down the centuries. There is a matter known as the "second facsimile" or "duplicate facsimile."

A theta being takes a picture of the memory of a GE and carries it as a record. A GE takes a picture of the memories of theta beings and carries those. Thus there can be many second facsimiles of past deaths for the same period of time. One should not be surprised at "discovering" five past deaths all occurring in the same span of years. Some will be second facsimiles. A maximum of two, for that period, will be actual incidents. One death happened to the theta being using another GE line, the other happened to the GE. They will be in different places and at different times.

Second facsimiles are "photographs" of the memories of another. They are still pictures usually. Their characteristic is that they show up with only two or three pictures of some long-ago situation. As they are "pictures" of charge and age and everything else, they will show up on an E-Meter as charged incidents. But when one tries to audit them, they change into the basic incident—the actual one—the "pictures" vanishing. The existence of a real facsimile in the GE or the theta being will restimulate and hold, as locks, pictures taken from former theta beings and GEs. Any death registering or any incident registering on an E-Meter for a certain period in the GE line tells you that there is a real incident in that area. Hunting for the real one, you may find some of these second facsimiles. These usually evaporate when touched and the actual incident is quickly found.

This matter is mentioned because auditors are sometimes puzzled by shifting dates on an E-Meter or incidents simultaneously occurring where they should not. An auditor, merely by pursuing the matter, automatically sorts out the second facsimiles which may be there and finds the actual facsimiles which must be audited.

Contact between a theta being and a GE must be very intimate for a photograph to be taken of the other's facsimiles. Or two beings must be in almost hypnotic rapport for the matter to occur. The facsimiles, themselves, do not shift from one to the other. One being simply sees and makes a "picture" of the facsimile of another when that other has the facsimile in restimulation. Any auditor has "seen" his preclear's incidents.

HERE IS A MAP SHOWING THE RELATIONSHIP OF THE GE TO THETA BEINGS:

—⊢————⊢— Unbroken line of PROTOPLASM through time, forming family generations, father, son, grandson, great-grandson, etc., etc.

------------ GENETIC ENTITY, choosing different lines of protoplasm from generation to generation, completely random in choice.

ooooooooooo THETA BEING, choosing MEST bodies at random, generation to generation without regard to the GE or protoplasm line.

xxxxxxxxxxxxx Another THETA BEING line.

ooooooooooooo
------------ Combination of PROTOPLASM LINE, THETA BEING, GENETIC ENTITY, a combination necessary to a Homo sapiens. These particular individualities will probably never meet in this combination again. No theta being or GE ordinarily continues in the same family line or with each other. Thus combinations are entirely random and new in each new generation. Thus the theta being can be audited as itself, but will be found in company with different GEs each generation. Thus GEs are found with different protoplasm lines each generation.

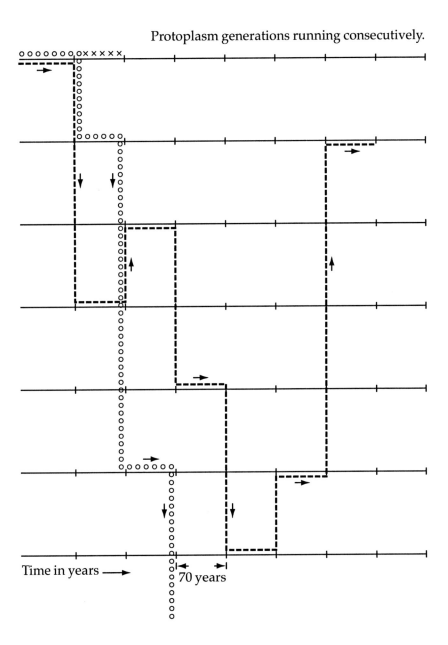

Protoplasm generations running consecutively.

Time in years ⟶   70 years

ASSUMPTIONS

ASSUMPTION is the name given to the act of a theta being taking over a MEST body. This is occasionally found to be part of the record of the GE, strong enough to be audited. It is the sensation of being taken over thoroughly and sometimes contains the shock of contact. The Assumption takes place, in most cases, just prior to birth for every GE generation.

Evidently, theta being Assumption is recent on Earth. It is rare to find a theta being coming to Earth thirty-five thousand years ago, rarer to find one earlier. Seventy thousand years ago is the present earliest arrival of a theta being on Earth. In a great many cases, the preclear (for the awareness of awareness of the preclear *is* the theta being) will be found to have arrived on Earth for the first time only a few hundred years ago. E-Meter reaction occurs in the GE line on these Assumptions and the auditor should be careful to differentiate whether he is reading for the GE or the preclear himself.

The GE takes a poor outlook on Assumptions. But in reality, it is not much different to the GE to be taken over by a theta being than by a new epicenter developed in the past generation.

There is a smothering peculiar to Assumption, from the viewpoint of the GE, which is followed by a fear of being caught, a desire to hide, a wonderingness at this nothingness which hit him and wrapped him up.

DEPARTURES

The GE stays with a dying body to the complete end and then soars upward and obtains a downview of the dead. This is routine. In that the anaten of death deepens as the end nears, and goes deeper than in any other incident, an auditor may leave the end of a death unaudited by carelessness.

The theta being leaves earlier than the GE and the GE sometimes records the DEPARTURE of the theta being before the GE itself DEPARTS from the dying.

There are conditional Departures of both in bad accidents and operations.

THE THETA

"The theta being
is the principal target of
the auditor."

BEING

Chapter Five

THE
THETA BEING

*T*HE THETA BEING is the principal target of the auditor.

The preclear IS the theta being.

The main thing wrong with any preclear is that he cannot disentangle himself from entities and somatic entities, from demon circuits and MEST bodies. He wants to know WHO he is and WHERE he is. A common complaint from a preclear is that somebody won't let him be himself. The joke of this is that the preclear doesn't know who HIMSELF is, much less why he can't be allowed to be HIM.

Take any preclear, using Concept Running, Motivator, Overt and DED, and you will find him instantly in the midst of dozens of engrams if you ask him to run the concepts "I am myself," "You are yourself," "What is my name?" "Who am I?" and similar concepts which attempt to single out his identity.

The only reason why a person becomes aberrated about other people is that he cannot distinguish between himself and others. You find preclears—and auditors too—who go around thinking themselves burdened with the facsimiles of others, who become restimulated and then try to run the engrams of others to cool the restimulation.

IDENTIFICATION OF THE REAL "I" IS THE SURE CURE FOR IDENTIFICATION OF SELF WITH OTHERS AND OTHERS WITH OTHERS.

WHO is the preclear? He is the theta being.

HOW does one really de-aberrate and clear a preclear? By clearing the theta being.

By running genetic entity incidents, by cleaning up present life, by running past deaths, the auditor can get rid of psychosomatics by the bale for the preclear. The auditor can practically rebuild the body. He can clarify thought by taking away pains restimulated by thinking. He can do a thousand thousand marvels never before possible here on Earth—or anywhere else for that matter.

But when he has done all these things, often at great labor, what does he have? He has a composite being, good enough to be called Homo novis—a theta-animated MEST body possessed of new and desirable attributes. That doesn't mean he has the preclear cleared. That doesn't mean he has located the preclear for the preclear and restored an ultimate self-determinism. It means the auditor has done well. The auditor has made what we are calling a MEST Clear—a good, sane, rational MEST being about a skyscraper higher than Homo sapiens. But in that Homo sapiens is a pretty horrible thing to be, this isn't good enough, not nearly good enough.

This Homo novis is limited in his self-determinism by all the economic and social restrictions of an aberrated society. He is not free of food, clothing or shelter. He dies when you get him too cold, he perishes when the oxygen content drops too low. He is living in a tolerance band which keeps him cramped to the face of one second-rate planet in a tenth-rate system, prey to all the ill will that blows. Is this being free or self-determined? Maybe he is good enough to overlord his fellows into a security for himself never before possible. But that is his only real route toward security. He must fight and command for his three squares, he must use police protection in order to keep himself free of bullet holes and bumper marks. Compared to a Homo sapiens, Homo novis is very high and godlike. Compared to a truly self-determined being, Homo novis is an ant ready to die under anybody's misstep.

CHAPTER FIVE • THE THETA BEING

This universe is a rough universe. It is a terrible and deadly universe. Only the strong survive it, only the ruthless can own it. Given one weak spot, a being cannot long endure it. For this universe will search it out and enlarge it and fester and probe it, until that weak spot is a festering wound so large that the being is engulfed by his own sores.

Fighting this battle for survival, and fight it he must, a being in the MEST universe cannot seem to afford decency or charity or ethics. He cannot afford any weakness, any mercy. The moment he does, he is lost—for he is surrounded by chilled, coarse rock and molten energy which, no matter the state of aberration of his social surroundings, will engulf him instantly that he ceases to obey the very least laws of MEST.

This is a universe of force. It is not a universe of reason. Brutal, unthinking, without decency or mercy, MEST force awaits with punishment any being with any weakness.

The possession of a MEST body is a liability. For through that body, the being can be given pain, can be regimented by the routine demands of eating and care from harm until at the very, very highest, he can be but a puppet dancing to the spin of some unthinking planet under the strong glare of a remote and careless sun. Under these conditions, a being—burdened with the care and liability of a body, made uncertain by an unknowingness—bows to strange and non-existent gods, resorts to terrible makeshifts in lieu of justice, cringes before the mightier bomb, the sharper blade.

You have examined an engram. A standard engram is simply the collision of the body with the MEST universe with sufficient impact to produce the confusion of attention known as "unconsciousness."

Should you care to make a test, just run "care of the body" as a total therapy. You will discover that by running out the postulates of a preclear about his body and its care and his injunctions and insistences to others that they care for their bodies, you can produce soaring changes in tone.

An entire book can be written concerning this therapy. An entire book has been written about it—the first book in Dianetics.

This therapy could be styled, "The efforts of a theta being to reconcile the frailty of a MEST body with the ethics of a theta being." They do not reconcile, these two. Schopenhauer, Zeno and names without number in philosophy have been trying to make this reconciliation for eons. One says, "Defeat it all and die, for only by dying can you defeat it." Another says, "You can't win, therefore the only victory is in refusing to try to win."

Christianity and a million other -anities have struggled with this problem and the result is a potpourri of answers, none of which reconcile the problem: You have a soul—it goes off somewhere, you don't know about it. You are a soul—you don't know about it.

Today we live in a vast cult called "Worship the Body." Medical doctors, schoolteachers, parents, traffic officers, the whole society unites into this war cry, "Care for the body." This stems from the ignorance that the body is all that one has, that he will have just one body, that his total devotion is the care of that body.

A body is a vegetable. It is not even a sentient vegetable, for it lacks perception in the whole theta range. Like any vegetable, it grows from seed and has habit patterns which help it survive. And like any vegetable, one way or another, it gets used by others.

Early theta beings saw MEST bodies acting and being as though they were self-motivated. This was a curiosity. The early theta being did not know that these MEST bodies depended wholly for their wits upon the guidance of a decayed theta being. The bodies looked like entities of considerable force and skill. The theta beingness of them was hidden and unapparent.

Thus, even theta beings have been fooled by MEST bodies.

A MEST body, whether it belongs to the race of Man or the race of ants, is yet but an animated vegetable. Given a theta being to guide it, it becomes part of a composite such as Homo sapiens.

64

Here we have a theta being, decayed into unknowingness, devoted to the care of a MEST body. The "I" of this body, the actual volition of it, all its wits and skills, are theta things derived from the guidance of a theta being. By itself the body would live, walk around, react, sleep, kill and direct an existence no better than that of a field mouse or a zombie. Put a theta being over it and it becomes possessed of ethics and morals and direction and goals and the ability to reason. It becomes this strange thing called Homo sapiens, a being above animals and yet an animal.

Give this MEST body a psychotic theta being and you get a sort of Frankenstein's monster. Give this MEST body a nearly unconscious theta being and you get a zombie.

The body is a carbon-oxygen engine which runs at 98.6°F. The theta being is the engineer running this engine in a Homo sapiens. There is already an entity running this engine, the GE, but there is here only a total devotion to avoiding pain, seeking survival factors of the meanest sort, begetting new MEST bodies. Every cell in that body has its own theta. The GE is theta. A theta being is something else entirely.

In the first place, the theta being came into being without the need of a MEST body, without the need of motors. It is close to a perpetual motion machine in that it can create energy and impulses. It thinks without facsimiles, it can act without experience, it can know simply by being. When we have talked of "optimum performance" in Dianetics or Scientology, we have talked about the actual top-level capabilities of the theta being, not the capabilities of the MEST being. Early work in Dianetics treats of the composite called Homo sapiens and treats that composite for what it is—an identity of several parts which act in greater or lesser coordination. You can go right on treating this composite being as a unit, you can go right on treating him and getting results for which you will be praised. But you must know that you are not treating the actual identity when you treat the MEST body. You are furthering a composite and actually you are subscribing to the international cult called "Care of the Body."

You can, at your own choice, go on living with and processing this composite known as Homo sapiens and create Homo novis. You can use Dianetics to make hitherto impossible strides. But be advised that in this choice you are living with paradoxes which no philosopher in all the ages ever reconciled—the injustice of death, the depravity of human beings as in Plato, the penalty of assisting another, the impossibility of having good ARC and survival too, the liability of being kind and merciful and every "unanswerable" religious paradox known. You, by persisting in yesterday's reality are persisting, then, in problems which have never been resolved with the factors accepted. You are demanding of a MEST-theta composite that he be self-determined when every zephyr from a hard universe contains death for him and can turn him like a top. You are demanding that he be "careful" when his only salvation is to be carefree. You are saddling him with all the unanswered riddles of an aberrated life in an aberrated world. And you are condemning a preclear to the dwindling spiral—for the theta being, as part of the composite, decays fast and soon dies forever in the rigid apathy of MEST.

Thus this data is given you. In lieu of this data, the only thing which could be given Man is the answering salute to the gladiators—they who are about to die.

As an auditor, the choice is yours to make—the paradoxes or the answer. I would not give you this data unless it can be demonstrated on any preclear with ease. And I would not give it to you unless you needed it.

Here it is.

CAPABILITIES

"The theta being, on his own,
can instill anything on the emotional
range into another being, for each
emotion is a wavelength and
wave characteristic."

OF THE
THETA BEING

Chapter Six

CAPABILITIES OF THE THETA BEING

*T*HE CAPABILITIES of the theta being cannot at this time be set down in a full sweep of data.

In the first place, it would be unfair to tomorrow to detail in writing the exact constitution of a theta being. For by just that much could he be predicted and brought again into a low state. The auditor does not have to know too much of these full capabilities. The preclear will discover them for himself in processing.

But there are a few data necessary to auditing and these are set forth:

A theta being is capable of emitting a considerable electronic flow. This is not done by using facsimiles, but is actually a creation of the motion which we now know as "electricity." A theta being produces considerable voltage and amperage, enough to give somebody a very bad shock, to put out his eyes or cut him in half.

The theta being, on his own, can instill anything on the emotional range into another being, for each emotion is a wavelength and wave characteristic.

A theta being does not use facsimiles to think or act. He does "mock-ups" of the situation and by examining the "mock-up" knows how something works or what should be done with a situation. His memory is by "pervasion"—which is to say, by pervading again the area of the data—or by "approximation." He is not stimulus-response.

Facsimiles are accumulated by a theta being at will, discarded at will, much as a man collects stamps.

Theta beings can rip chains of facsimiles away from other theta beings. This is not done as a therapy, but as an outright prankish theft.

The identity of a theta being is not based on his memory of events, but on an actual knowledge of identity.

A theta being can be rendered unconscious by wave action. He can be hypnotized. He can be made to sleep. He can be made to possess facsimiles and use them. He can be aberrated in such fashion so as to forget his identity. He is subject to all the laws and rules of thought, emotion and effort as described in Dianetics and Scientology—with the difference that, fairly Clear, he has enormous choice in their use.

A theta being can be de-aberrated by ridding him of his chains of facsimiles and restoring to him his knowledge of identity.

A theta being can enjoy existence and emotional impact, he can plan and act. His activities lie above 8.0 on the Tone Scale. He is very high aesthetically and devotes most of his time to aesthetics.

Theta beings associate socially with theta beings and have a high sense of justice.

A theta being can be made visible by certain electronic flows. He can be pinned down by certain flows. The wavelengths of these flows are not known to Homo sapiens at this time and methods of emission of them have not been invented on Earth.

MEST beings of the class of Homo sapiens are composite beings motivated by a theta being, entities, the GE and the environment. MEST beings, fallen away from being theta beings, incapable of regaining a theta state in the absence of Dianetics, dislike theta beings (whom we will call THETANS from here on, meaning a theta being who has not been forced to have a MEST body). MEST beings, trying to inhabit an area of thetans, are commonly balked and fought by the thetans. And the MEST beings then begin to trap and harass the thetans and will use them to motivate new bodies when the thetans have been reduced to little or nothing in power. The *they* which you will discover in incidents are MEST beings. The current Homo sapiens is a *they*. MEST beings (amnesia and a MEST body) attack thetans who menace them. Thetans can kill MEST bodies by throwing a charge at them. Thus a war develops between thetans and MEST beings. Given electronics and hitherto unconquered thetans, MEST beings can and have won.

Thetans communicate by telepathy. They can move material objects by throwing an energy flow at them. They can travel at very high speeds. They are not bound by atmospheres or temperatures.

Thetans quarrel with each other by showing each other facsimiles or throwing energy flows at each other, but they are not very quarrelsome.

Thetans do not die. They grow, in that there are young and old thetans. Decaying, they obtain MEST bodies and eventually pass out in the form of a solid, apathetic slumber.

A thetan can feel pain. He can be crippled and dismembered, but this requires force which would blow half a town off the map.

Thetans live on some planets. They consider these to be "outside the MEST universe," by which they mean outside areas inhabited by the composite beings—the "races" which use electronics and need bodies.

A thetan, brought low enough to have a MEST body, may consider that he has been trapped by "time warps" or that his universe is another dimension or some such thing. This is not the case. Thetans live in the same time stream with the difference that they can alter concepts of time and get future or past at will. It is the thetan who is altering his concept, not the time that is changing. So don't go off on wild chases after fourth and fifth dimensions, time warps and other time-space universes: teleportation makes it look like these exist for the thetan. There is more to this, but you don't really need it in processing.

There are two states of "Theta Clear": One of these is a CLEARED THETAN, from whom all incidents would be removed. The other is the THETAN cleared of a necessity to have a MEST body. When we say "Theta Clear" we mean the latter.

A thetan is somewhat bound-in here on Earth because of the existence of other system forces. Probably, with a few thetans active, this planet will be much less calm and orderly. Probably Homo sapiens will use electronics someday to re-trap thetans who are bothering him. But if Homo sapiens has the techniques for getting free himself, some miracle might avert this. Possibly a handful of thetans will someday become alarmed at the worries and efforts of Homo sapiens and try to throw the remaining race into a super-controlled slavery. All that is speculation. But it is not a speculation that life will become much more interesting on this planet. It is doubtful if the thetans will pull off the ultimate trick—simply knocking out the atmosphere of the planet—that "clears" everybody after a fashion. There is nothing as wild in the books of Man as will probably happen here on Earth. And it will happen and be allowed to happen simply because all this is so incredible that nobody will even think of stopping it until it is far, far too late. Its incredibility is its best safeguard, so you needn't bother to convince anybody who doesn't want to believe it. It took the medical profession two and a half years to catch on to prenatals. People getting cleared of bodies don't need any such time lag. And so, may I make this simple request: Don't get spectacular until a few of the boys make it. You don't want to be lonesome—and you'll need reinforcements if a war gets declared on thetans here. The preclear may think he can do it alone if he gets cleared of a body. He'll need more help and company than he thinks.

So, again, as a final note on this chapter: Let's not go upsetting governments and putting on a show to "prove" anything to Homo sapiens for a while. It's a horrible temptation to knock off hats at fifty yards and read books a couple of countries away and get into the rotogravure section and the Hearst weeklies. But you'll just make it tough on somebody else who is trying to get across this bridge.

Let sleeping sapiens snore in the bulk for yet a while. Then meet someplace and decide what to do about him and his two-penny wars, his insane and his prisons. Tell people who want to invalidate all this, "Your criticism is very just. It's only fantasy." Cure up the lame and the halt and the incompetent with whatever display of technique you need. Protect Theta Clearing until there are a few.

HISTORY
OF THE

"Thetans like facsimiles
just like a Homo sapiens
likes TV."

THETA LINE

Chapter Seven

HISTORY OF THE THETA LINE

THE HISTORY OF the theta line is long and interesting. All you really want to know of it, however, is how much of it applies to your preclear. You will be pleased to discover that this is relatively little, a snap of the fingers in time compared to what could be.

The whole track seems to be about 70 trillion years long.

Thetans like facsimiles just like a Homo sapiens likes TV. A thetan can take a facsimile and inspect it. He likes to collect them like a bibliophile collects books. Any thetan has purloined packages of facsimiles from other thetans, just like schoolboys take pictures of champions away from each other. Thus your thetan has two things: He has his own record of real experience, of things which actually happened to him. And he has whole banks of "second facsimiles" or "photographs" he has taken from other thetans' banks.

Second facsimiles are complete pictures. They will show up with charge on an E-Meter because they also contain the "charge notation." But the moment you locate the fact that the whole bank of second facsimiles was taken from another being, the preclear stops using them as experience and they no longer show up on the E-Meter. The characteristic of the second facsimile on the E-Meter, then, is to show up for a short time and then, identified as from a "borrowed" bank, not register anymore.

79

The best way to knock out second facsimile banks is to run out of the preclear incidents of "borrowing" facsimiles. He'll have many of these.

A preclear, needing a motivator for some overt act he has done, will start to use a second facsimile as the motivator. It will even give him somatics. A preclear may have as many as eight banks he is using. Identify seven of them as "borrowed" banks and you have him operating, then, on his own bank. This is the step necessary to get him running on his own actual track.

Sometimes you may find that he has used a second facsimile so much that it has to be run. Run, it shows up as two or three still pictures, not as a moving picture.

The only truly important facsimiles are those which actually happened to the thetan himself, not what he borrowed.

You can plot out, as you wish, the whole track. Incidents given here in this volume (or variations of them) will be found on this track.

A common history of the theta line, as applied to your preclear, starts with his SEPARATION FROM THE MAIN BODY OF THETA, continues through HOME UNIVERSE, runs into his ENTRAPMENT BY MEST BEINGS and then through life as we know it—with its cycle of birth, MEST body living, death, between-lives wipe-out and birth again.

The thetan lives his life in segments, called SPIRALS. As he goes through the MEST universe, he is involved in a series of spirals, each one less in terms of years, ordinarily, than the last. The first spiral, which occurred approximately 76 trillion years ago, might have been as long as a trillion years. But the next spiral after that was a little shorter. Succeeding spirals, each one, shortened. The present spiral for most people is about forty thousand years long, although many are on a longer spiral than this and not a few are on a very short spiral. The length of this spiral might serve to indicate how much longer the thetan can continue.

By a spiral would be meant a more or less continuous cycle of action. A life in a MEST body is a variety of cycles. It is not a spiral, for the preclear's knowingness often extends to earlier bodies. The first big cycle would be, at its probable longest, 76 trillion years. This would be subdivided into spirals, any one of which might comprise more than one lifetime. Spirals could be subdivided into "lives," such as the current life which is only one division of the current spiral. A whole spiral can get into restimulation in some earlier period, just as a past life can get into restimulation in this life. The incidents contained in that whole spiral, then, would be quite important. Sometimes a spiral has ended suddenly and earlier than scheduled for a preclear. This has remained to him as a very bad shock. It would be like a past death, but of a very great magnitude. The beginning of this spiral finds the being thinking he is new, with universes to conquer. And the end of the spiral finds him practically expiring, even as a thetan.

The overt acts of the thetan are "Nipping," by which he harasses other thetans; "Nipping" MEST beings, which usually kills them dead much to the thetan's surprise; "Blanketing" of MEST bodies for sexual thrill and other purposes; trapping other thetans after one has become a MEST being; and the usual variety of overt acts common on Earth.

None of this is very complicated as a history. It is made to *look* complicated by the existence of borrowed banks, entities and "cover-up" actions by the preclear. The main task of the auditor is to get the preclear to identify himself as himself and to identify the actual track of himself. The rest is easy.

TYPES OF INCIDENTS

"What does it take

to aberrate a thetan?"

ON THE
THETA LINE

Chapter Eight

TYPES OF INCIDENTS ON THE THETA LINE

HE TYPES OF INCIDENTS found on the theta line are somewhat different than the auditor has been accustomed to running in present life processing. The elements contained in those incidents are the same: thought, emotion, effort, counter-thought, counter-emotion, counter-effort, attention units and counter-units. The emphasis, however, is upon attention units and counter-units.

The reason for this is rather obvious. How would you go about nearly killing an almost immortal being? It would require about the heaviest force possible. The Tone Scale above 2.0 contains perception. Below 2.0 there is little or no perception beyond attention units. Here is the occluded case. The individual himself may be running on a higher harmonic of his occluded tone, but the incidents which must be run to restore his perception in incidents are all too heavy to contain much in the way of perception. Hence, the tracking of attention units and the skills necessary to that are the requisites in running theta-track incidents. Further, so heavy are these facsimiles that one must be very conversant with Technique 80, for the incidents hang up when the motivator is run too long or when the overt or DED is run too long. (Old-time incidents were said to go into recession. This is because they had an overt or a motivator, opposite from them, which had to be run.)

The auditor never really understands apathy, fear or anger until he has run the heavy facsimiles of the theta line. It is not that they affect the preclear more strongly—they do not. It is that they are so heavy, they can be like so much glue or hardwood. Reversing to the opposite incident, to the overt from the motivator, to the motivator from the overt, alone makes it possible to run the theta line.

One might have known for a very long time how far back this theta line went and how serious were the incidents upon it. But it would have done him no good to know about these incidents. For without Attention Unit Running, which I developed only a short time ago, the incidents would not be runnable at all.

There were two ways of running a case: One was to unburden it until the natural resurgence of the individual keyed-out the lower, heavier incidents. The other was to run the incidents no matter how heavy they were. The theta line, then, could not be audited at all until Attention Unit Running and Overt Acts had been developed and refined for auditor application. The first method of unburdening is the one which auditors have been doing wholly, whether they realized it or not. The other one of cleaning up the incidents themselves, the very bottom basics of the chains, has not been in use because it couldn't be. Thus Dianetics was kept to one life until such time as the entire mechanical aspect of the lower track could be examined and techniques developed for resolving it. Of course, these techniques, if they resolve heavy incidents, resolve lighter ones as well. And so a revolution in processing can be announced which, if you *must* process only the current life, will resolve it in most cases in five or ten hours of processing. If it doesn't resolve, then the auditor simply doesn't know 80 and that's all there is to it.

Despite the fact that they are heavy, that they are strange, theta-line incidents are easy to audit *if* the auditor knows 80. If the incidents are very hard to run, then the auditor *doesn't* know 80.

There is just one warning about theta-line incidents: You are auditing the theta "body," not the MEST body. It is theoretically possible to run an incident out of the theta being which is too much for the MEST body. A MEST body which has a weak heart had better be audited in this lifetime only until his heart condition entirely vanishes. Some of the theta-line incidents kick back so hard against the MEST body that the preclear is sure he will not live through them. If the auditor doesn't balance the overt against the motivator in 80, if he runs one side too strongly and heavily and really drives in the somatic, he may be embarrassed by making a Theta Clear before his time—the body still lying about but not breathing.

The incidents themselves contain some things the auditor should know about. One doesn't have to be a nuclear physicist to understand these incidents, but the incidents are actually in the realm of nuclear physics.

The auditor must only know the following:

1. Strong electrical currents produce in the vicinity of their flow what are called MAGNETIC FIELDS. If you wrap an electrical wire around a bar of iron and run current through the wire, you have a magnet. When you put a new piece of iron near this magnet, the field of the magnet snaps the piece of iron up against the magnet.

2. In the vicinity of any strong current a wide FORCE FIELD exists. If this is intensified (by using great quantities of current) the force field may extend for hundreds of feet or even miles. A radio station is a sort of force field in that it reaches hundreds or thousands of miles out from it. It takes a radio set to pick up or contact this field strongly enough to get a good reaction out of it. But actually, this instant, thousands of stations throughout the world are sending force fields through your body. They are too minute to be measured or detected without receiving sets, but they are force fields just the same—wave impulses generated from a central point and extending far out from that point. If a station could generate a billion times the normal current a station uses, you would be able to contact that field physically, it would be so strong.

3. It is possible for a wave to act as a RETRACTOR. That is to say, it is possible for certain waves to pull back instead of push out. You turn a hose on somebody. This pushes him back. There can exist a wave which, if it were a hose, would pull you up to the nozzle instead of push you away. Thetans can put out such a retractor wave.

4. It is possible to rig up two or three or one standing POLE which is then activated with a current which will apply a very strong field to anyone in its vicinity. It is then possible to vary these fields to get various patterns of fields or to shift from one field to another to get various angles of attack on an object. A thetan sitting amongst such a field pattern can be very thoroughly battered and rendered unconscious. It is also possible to rig up a post which would have a retractor wave coming out of it and which would pull a thetan into the post and pin him there.

5. A FIELD is not always visible. "Black band" waves are the destructive waves. These are not visible and they light up nothing.

It may occur to the auditor that some of these incidents, as he hears them being run, are very reminiscent of the material which is commonly found among the insane in sanitariums. These people are quite given to chattering about fields and secret waves and telepathy and things being after them with electronic devices. The past ignorance consisted of treating anything an insane person had to say as nonfactual data. Today, many even say that one is insane to give thought to any such circumstances as occur on the theta line. An experienced auditor knows that to make the insane sane, it is necessary to run the incidents the insane person is dramatizing.

In a brilliant flash of insight, someday those in charge of sanitariums may see that the reason the insane chatter about electronics is that electronics are peculiarly adapted to tailor-making insanity and that electronics have been used for unthinkably long times to handle and control beings. Electronics alone can make a truly slave society. Those in charge of sanitariums, in view of the fact that their own figures show that electrical shocks do *no* good and have *no* beneficial effects upon patients, may someday wonder why they themselves are so violently psychotic on the subject of insisting that the insane be given electronics. Ah, you have it! Those in charge are doing a crude and ineffective dramatization of theta-line incidents. Electronics make slaves. If some of these electricity-obsessed, but electrically ignorant chaps who so gently shepherd our insane really *want* results—I can show them not just how to make a patient tractable, I can show them how to give him total amnesia so that he can then be taught like a child and may become useful in a few months. You can *really* wipe people out with electronics. Electric shock is so stupid and so childish that one wonders, one wonders.

So heavy is the concentration on electronics in the theta line, so closely connected with energy behavior is the anatomy of a theta being that only one trained in nuclear physics could have cracked this riddle. And with the data on this theta line, human treatment and the treatment of any life passes entirely into the hands of the electronics experts and out of the hands of the meddlers with minds whose training in electronics ends with knowing how to turn on an electric light and who yet have, at this writing, the only legislative passports into the craniums of the ill. The era has just begun. Using theta line data, data accumulated from preclears about electronics, wavelengths, practices and social customs, a handful of electronics experts could bring entire nations into their command with very little work—and those trained in yesterday would be completely powerless to stop or even detect that pervasion of command. This is regrettable, perhaps. Maybe all societies go this way. The atom bomb is a toy compared to a device which would turn into soulless slaves an entire city, an entire nation, an entire world. But instead of hiding this information, one should bring it to light. For if it goes underground, only then can it completely have its sway. One does not look for such an enslavement to occur, for you are reading the pages and the technologies which can and will defeat it.

Thus, in running your preclear, keep in mind that he has been, in the *past*, part of societies which had electronics down to a very fine point, which could control the very breathing of their subjects.

Recall that he may have been part of a town, for instance, in which any revolutionary, lazy or non-survival thought, if thought, would bring him, without will, to the steps of the local thought-police station. Remember, in processing your preclear, that for thousands of years he has played the game of enslaving and being enslaved. And the depths of control were such, the acts in that control were such, as to outsoar any mere imaginings from modern literature. Modern science fiction, even that, is a weak piker compared to the data of the past from which these writers of the future took their plots. A public couldn't stomach what really went on before Earth. Your preclear isn't able to stomach it—that's why he's forgotten it.

What does it take to aberrate a thetan? Thousands and thousands of volts, thousands of amperes, poured into destructive wavelengths and thrown straight in his face. What does it take to get him into a position where he can be aberrated? Trickery, treachery, lies.

Running electronics incidents is not difficult, not if you know 80. But there is a datum which must be repeated here, even though it belongs in *How to Audit*.

THE DEFINITION IN DIANETICS OF INVALIDATION:

INVALIDATION IS ANY THOUGHT, EMOTION OR EFFORT, COUNTER-THOUGHT, COUNTER-EMOTION OR COUNTER-EFFORT WHICH DENIES OR SMOTHERS THE THOUGHT, EMOTION OR EFFORT OF THE INDIVIDUAL.

By this definition, a man is invalidated by being struck by anything. If he is run into by a car, he is invalidated. Any accident invalidates him. Any force which he cannot conquer or oppose invalidates him.

Turn to the chart in your *Handbook for Preclears*. Here you see on the Chart of Attitudes, I KNOW, I AM, FAITH, etc. The more the force of an individual is cancelled out by counter-forces, the lower he drifts on this chart. Hit by strong forces, he conceives that he "isn't."

FAITH at the top of the chart turns to DISBELIEF at the bottom.

Turn a preclear loose into a heavy theta-line incident and what reaction do you get? You get bottom-chart reactions. That is to say, the force is such in the incident that he is utterly unable to combat it. Thus he conceives himself utterly invalidated. In such a wise he comes to express, in the incident, bottom-scale attitudes. He can't believe it, he isn't there, etc., etc. Run any theta-line incident with its heavy impacts and your preclear will immediately start to discredit it. Keep him at it, waive aside all his lacks of belief and other comments and soon the tone band will rise a notch or two. Keep the tone rising, using overts and motivators, and you eventually get perception and concepts.

Why do you think these theta-line incidents got lost? Why can't a man who has undergone a between-lives battering recall that he lived before? Invalidation by force is the answer. The Chart of Attitudes will give you your guide.

There is another thing you should know about these incidents and the emotional state of the preclear: He has become, in his own eyes, so degraded by force invalidation that he has devoted himself to this vegetable thing—the MEST body—as the last-ditch effort to control some part of the environment. HE is invalidated to nothing. So the BODY has to be something.

And there is something else, a scale you should have of invalidation:

CRITICISM AND COUNTER-CRITICISM are the overt and motivator invalidations on the thought level.

MIS-EMOTIONALISM AND COUNTER-MIS-EMOTIONALISM are the overt and motivator invalidations on the emotion level.

PHYSICAL FORCE AND COUNTER-PHYSICAL FORCE are the overt and motivator invalidations on the effort level.

In current or recent lives, thought, emotion and effort hang up on the early theta-line incidents. If you can't get a theta-line incident of the electronics type to unburden, run criticism and counter-criticism in the current life.

In general, you will find the preclear has been subjected, as a theta being, to enormous invalidation of all his force, power and natural attributes. The rise in tone potential in running the theta line is such that you can expect the preclear to go from low to high on the E-Meter after only one or two heavy electronics incidents have been run. But make sure they are theta line and that they happened to the thetan who is the preclear before you.

The intent of other beings was to make this preclear into a willing or unwilling, but at least obedient slave. Or to get him out of the area and keep him running away thereafter. Or to nail him into complete useless immobility. They wanted him to have good reaction to police threats (and most psychotics go psychotic immediately after a police interview, no matter how innocent it was). They wanted him to leave MEST bodies alone and respect them.

On his part, your preclear was part and parcel of many societies, took his role in efforts to conquer thetans after he had been conquered. He wanted MEST bodies to be respected now that he had one. He wanted his slaves to be obedient. He wanted beings he didn't like to start running and keep on running. Or barring that, to be immobile MEST thereafter. Your preclear has been guilty himself of any crime or action he protests occurred to him. For by his worry, he confesses that whether or not it happened to him, he did it to others.

Your preclear was basically good, happy, ethical and aesthetic before the contagion of the MEST universe got him. Then, still a thetan, he wasn't very good, but he was still trusting and ethical. Finally, when he had a body—well, look around.

SPECIFIC INCIDENTS

"The basic error a thetan
made was in considering a MEST
body something very special,
unmotivated by thetans."

ON THE
THETA LINE

Chapter Nine

SPECIFIC INCIDENTS ON THE THETA LINE

THE SPECIFIC INCIDENTS you must run on the theta line are directed solely, at this stage, toward attaining a voluntary and controlled separation between the MEST body and the theta body. This is much easier to do than you would at first believe and the incidents necessary to accomplishing it are relatively easy to comprehend and locate.

Remember that to create a Theta Clear, it is only necessary to bring the being up to a point where it can leave and return upon a MEST body. A Cleared Theta Clear would be a fully Cleared thetan, something so much higher on the Tone Scale than a MEST Clear or Theta Clear that it is difficult to comprehend. A Theta Clear, however, is not difficult to attain. Neither does it guarantee the release of all possible aberrations. A Theta Clear, some tones higher than anything known before, is yet subject to some aberration and will be until he attains the state of a Cleared Theta Clear. (Thus, don't invalidate somebody as a Theta Clear just because he doesn't act like a saint—he might even be more devilish than ever!)

Separation from the body! How the mystics have striven for this one! India and "join Nirvana" have given us "techniques" WHICH ARE GUARANTEED TO GLUE A THETAN TO A BODY AS THOUGH RIVETED AND TIED WITH IRON BANDS. So beware of mysticism and its techniques, yogism and its nonsense.

Your hardworking author has been over the jumps and through the hoops of more mysticism than is even suspected and on the ground where mysticism first hit Earth—India. And I can guarantee you that these practices and hopes are a sort of theta trap to keep men in their bodies, in apathy, ill and tied to superstition.

Theta Clearing is about as practical and simple as repairing a shoelace. It has nothing to do with hypnotism, voodooism, charlatanism, monkeyism or theosophy. Done, the thetan can do anything a stage magician can do in the way of moving objects around. But this isn't attained by holding one's breath or thinking "right" thoughts or voting Republican or any other superstitious or mystic practice.

So, which is the reason I've brought it up, rule out, auditor, any mumbo jumbo of mysticism or spiritualism. Rule out anything but good, solid, contactable incidents which are run wholly and entirely with the mechanical techniques of Dianetics with particular attention to 80.

The key chart of Theta Clearing is the Chart of Attitudes which you will find in the *Handbook for Preclears*. All the Straightwire is done from that chart.

Here are some incidents, more or less in the order that the auditor will find them and run them.

THE JACK-IN-THE-BOX

Here we have an invader trick, a method of trapping thetans. It is a facsimile scrambler. It is very early, not the earliest, only the earliest invader trick.

The thetan area is invaded by MEST beings. The thetans bother the MEST beings, "nipping" them, etc. The MEST beings use theta traps. One of these is to give to thetans pretty little boxes. These boxes contain a stack of pictures. As thetans are disposed to gather facsimiles, these pictures are very acceptable. The thetan looks over the pictures. He finds they are quite similar one to another. They show, each one, a picture of a box of pictures. When he replaces the lid the box explodes violently. He instinctively tries to dampen the explosion. He gets his aura of beingness full of pictures which are extremely confusing, being pictures of boxes of pictures.

The running of this incident is simple. One keeps the preclear's attention on the point of explosion, out from him. Of course, this point slams back at him every time he puts his attention on it. You will find a preclear with this in restimulation to be very curious about cereal boxes which have pictures of boxes of cereal which have pictures of boxes of cereal.

There may be several such incidents including being near such explosions.

*T*HE *O*BSESSION

This incident is the incident which gives one the feeling he *has* to have facsimiles in order to *know*. Actually, one doesn't need facsimiles. One thinks in concepts, approximations, pervasions. A fine control trick is to make one think he has to have facsimiles. This aberrates him and makes him easy to handle. Educational systems are locks on this. The incident is an electronic incident, very strong, and sometimes includes a great many source-points of energy directed against one's back. Just before it, one KNOWS. The force of the waves themselves, depressing one on the Chart of Attitudes, stops one from knowing.

This incident gives one an OBSESSION to have facsimiles, to steal facsimiles, to do anything to get facsimiles. One is actually trying to find what one lost in the incident and that was lost by force alone.

WARNING: DON'T EVER TRY TO RUN WORDS OR OTHER PERCEPTIONS OUT OF ANY ELECTRONIC INCIDENTS. WORDS ARE SELDOM INCLUDED IN THEM. COMMUNICATION IN SUCH AN ERA WAS USUALLY BY THOUGHT TRANSFER, NOT BY WORDS. THIS IS VERY IMPORTANT.

BORROWING

Thetans hold facsimiles very loosely. A high-scale thetan can pick up and discard facsimiles at will. Further, a thetan often steals the facsimile chains of another thetan as a result of the OBSESSION. Thus we will find, as the primary source of occlusion, the BORROWER.

A thetan puts a retractor beam on another thetan and starts to drag out his facsimiles. The victim feels like he is going to pieces. He, the victim, puts up a black screen to halt the outflow of his facsimiles. The Borrower counters by throwing a cone of force above and below the victim, pinning him between these two cones as though to squeeze him out. The black protecting screen usually can be held in place, but the facsimiles, like smoke, trickle out around the black screen and to the Borrower.

The most remarkable thing about this incident is the *slowness* with which facsimiles seem to run out. Each facsimile has its own time tab. No matter how rapidly they are leaving, these time tabs give the *illusion* of a very long time. Running up and down one's time track often gives this illusion. Thus, although the outflow from the victim may be done in seconds, it may seem to take years. The preclear often protests against running this incident because "It takes too long." Actually, it takes very little time.

Naturally, on the Borrower, the overt act must be gotten as well as the motivator—as in all incidents run. If you don't get the reverse to what you are running, incidents hang up. In the Borrower, the overt is the same as the motivator as the incidents are very similar, but with reverse action. Run the preclear as the Borrower and the victim both, one after the other, back and forth, in order to get up the whole of each.

This incident is the source of fear of losing one's facsimiles, the source of occlusion and the collapse of time tracks.

NIPPING

NIPPING is a practice much beloved by thetans.

They send out two energy streams, like hands, and slap both sides of a victim's head. This mildly shocks a thetan to which it is done. It can kill a MEST body. This slap is notable for causing ringing in the ears. This predates any invader. It is very early. It also postdates invaders.

In running Nips, one is running something very important. For it is a basic on holding on to a MEST body. As in all incidents, when you run the motivator, run the overt afterwards, or vice versa.

BLANKETING

This incident consists of throwing oneself, as a thetan, over another thetan or over a MEST body. BLANKETING is done to obtain an emotional impact or even to kill.

It is strongest in sexual incidents, where the thetan throws two MEST bodies together in the sexual act in order to experience their emotions. This sexual lust comes from the "Halver." It is very, very strong and is very restimulative in the running. Here is where the Second Dynamic becomes aberrated. There is considerable frenzy in these incidents. This is also basic on fastening on to a MEST body or holding a MEST body or protecting MEST bodies. It is an overt act. It has DEDs later than it in almost any sexual activity on the part of the preclear. At times, a thetan will Blanket a MEST body and hold it so that it can be attacked by another MEST body motivated by another thetan. Later, the thetan, having committed this overt act, will start protecting MEST bodies from attacks by thetans. This gives a person great antipathy toward seeing men and women together, lays in a basic on jealousy, etc.

There is a steep emotional curve in Blanketing. First there is the high excitement, then orgasm, then—for the bodies—contentment or apathy as the case may be. This drop affects the thetan strongly and he gets fastened to the bodies and it takes some while to separate himself at times. These incidents make the future fixation on MEST bodies possible. Thus Freud had something when he blamed sex, but sex is far from the whole story.

THE BASIC ERROR A THETAN MADE WAS IN CONSIDERING A MEST BODY SOMETHING VERY SPECIAL, UNMOTIVATED BY THETANS. HE DID NOT REALIZE THAT ANY MEST (HUMAN) BODY IS RUN BY A DECAYED THETAN. IN THIRSTING TO RUN MEST BODIES AND IN CONTACTING THEM, HE THOUGHT HE WAS CONTACTING A CELLULAR BODY WHEREAS HE WAS ACTUALLY CONTACTING A THETAN AND A BODY. HE DESIRED TO GO INTO ARC, WITHOUT KNOWING IT, WITH A DECADENT THETAN WHO HAD A MEST BODY. THAT EVERY MEST (HUMAN-LIKE) BODY HAD A DECAYED THETAN ON IT WAS UNKNOWN TO THETANS UNTIL NOW. THIS ACCOUNTS FOR THE ENORMOUS "KICKBACK" RECEIVED BY A THETAN WHEN HE NIPS A MEST BODY OR BLANKETS ONE. THE BODY NEVER DID HAVE THAT POWER. THE DECAYED THETAN DID. RESPECT OF MEST BODIES, THEN, WAS ENTIRELY MISPLACED. THIS IS THE PRIMARY ERROR THETANS MADE.

THE HALVER

Don't think thetans were only abused.

When MEST bodies tried to invade and take over an area, they usually wound up enslaved to the thetans in that area. And the thetans used them horribly. The invader sometimes came in with electronics, his only defense against a thetan. The thetan quite ordinarily took the electronics over and used them on the MEST bodies.

One of the processes thetans used on MEST bodies was a HALF-LIGHT, HALF-BLACK gun which shot out a wave. Half of this wave, usually the black, hit the right side of the victim's body. The other half, in the same explosion, usually the light side, hit the left side of the victim. This had the effect of causing him to be two people. It is also the basic on half-paralysis such as strokes. There was not always regularity in this incident. Sometimes it was the practice to shoot the victim one way and then turn him around and shoot him the other, sometimes the sides and head as well.

The HALVER was rigged up with religious symbols and it truly lays in religion. There is a devil on one side, a symbol carried in the light, angels on the other side. Sometimes it was very fancy and was complicated with dolls in the shape of nudes, angels, devils, strung on wires to slide and dance.

It did terrible things to the victim: It gave him a conflict, one side with the other, one being good, the other being bad. It gave him sexual compulsion all mixed up with religious compulsion so that an overdose of indulgence would send him to church, sometimes into a life of crime. It was a control factor used to keep the community fighting itself.

The Halver lies as a basic under sexual malpractice, under religious fervor. It shows up in almost every preclear as being in chronic restimulation. It is the one the auditor runs as an overt act when the preclear has a sexual or religious motivator.

Remember that the restimulation of a motivator when one does an overt act is not natural, but a consequence of having a body and implants about bodies. You will find some of this "you do wrong, you'll get it right back" in the Halver and similar incidents.

FACSIMILE ONE

This incident is in everyone's bank, either as a second facsimile or as an original. Only in the latter case should it be run.

It is called FACSIMILE ONE because it is the first proven-up whole track incident which, when audited out of a long series of people, was found to eradicate such things as asthma, sinus trouble, chronic chills and a host of other ills.

It has a verbal content in most cases.

It is quite varied when found as an original. For in this case, it happened to the preclear in the last ten or twenty thousand years. It was originally laid down in this galaxy about one million years ago.

The "Coffee-Grinder" (which might be an alternate name for it) is leveled at the preclear and a push-pull wave is played over him, first on his left side, then on his right, and back and forth from side to side, laying in a bone-deep somatic which cannot be run unless you recognize it as a vibration, not the solid board it seems to be. When this treatment is done, the preclear is dumped in scalding water, then immediately in ice water. Then the preclear is put in a chair and whirled around. He was quite swollen after the pummeling of the waves and was generally kept in a badly run (but quite modern) hospital for a few days. Sometimes he was given several treatments and after the first one would report back on schedule for the next.

Fac One was an outright control mechanism, invented to cut down rebel raids on invader installations. It was probably designed by the Fourth Invader and used by him in its original state and "ritual" for a considerable time. It gave him a nice, non-combative, religiously insane community.

THE MOST IMPORTANT PART OF FAC ONE APPERTAINS TO ITS "SUMMONS TO COURT." This was a sick quiver installed in the stomach area by the Coffee-Grinder during the first part of the incident. The Coffee-Grinder laid in "baps" on the pineal and other points, but almost knocked out the pineal potential forever and relegated its actions to the pituitary. It knocked in every other glandular point. And these same "baps" were used against the vagus nerve to give what everyone knows as an "anxiety stomach," uncontrolled bowel action, etc., etc. The invader wanted people to report when sent for. Thus the context (which must never be run until the emotion and effort are reduced) when the vagus area was "bapped" concentrates on getting the preclear to report quickly when summoned and makes him terrified of arrest, of courts, of other legal hocus-pocus. Thus criminal action against individuals, or sometimes any legal action, interrupts the glandular system, gives an anxiety reaction which has no equal anywhere else on the track. Experienced police know this sudden hitherto inexplicable collapse of the criminal and his feeling that he would rather be dead than simply arrested.

One cannot exaggerate the effect of Fac One in the legal department. A check on psychotics recently showed five, taken at random, to have been "triggered" by a threat of arrest a short time before the psychotic break occurred. This is Fac One at work.

The Coffee-Grinder is a two-handled portable machine which, when turned, emits a heavy push-pull electronic wave in a series of stuttering "baps." It is violently restimulated by what construction companies call "widow-makers"—pneumatic drills of the kind used to tear up pavement. The sound is not dissimilar. Fac One, not silicosis, is responsible for the mortality of workers assigned to these drills on construction projects.

In the original version, the invaders operated these machines while wearing hoods and goggles, not unlike "hot papa" suits used today on aircraft carriers. The victim was placed behind a black gauze curtain, but in running Fac One the preclear usually catches glimpses of the Coffee-Grinder and the users. Some people who wear horn-rimmed glasses are found to be solidly in the operator valence in Fac One. Such people are lean and hectic. Some persons whose faces are "swollen" and who have a "dumpy" build, who are given to asthma, are found solidly in the victim valence.

The invader gratuitously left these machines around for the yokels. Believing that the treatment was vital to get to heaven or some such thing, the yokels practiced on each other, found new victims and generally spread the implant around. Trouble with the machines the invader left around was that they "backfired" while they were working, sending out a ray into the chest of the operator to restimulate him, the yokel operator not suspecting that the machine was hitting anything else but his victim. And the yokel operator had neither goggles nor a "hot papa" suit. One of these unskilled operators lasted sometimes as long as forty victims before he collapsed from restimulation himself. The "backfire" characteristic of the machines left around also inhibited the local people from using electronic "handguns" and "rifles," thus killing off guerrillas who sought to attack the invader, for electronic weapons had a flashback against the user.

Fac One deteriorated down the years, became quite varied and with the colonization of Earth about thirty-five thousand years ago (or up to seventy thousand in a very few cases), when used, Fac One was quite non-standard. But it has been used on Earth against some preclears.

About a hundred and some thousand years ago, the Halver was substituted for Fac One as much more efficient, much quicker and less destructive of personnel and more creative of slave-like devotion. Thus the preclear is certain to have the Halver as an original. You will also get an E-Meter drop on Fac One. Be sure to ask if it is original or a borrowed facsimile. And don't forget its overt act is Fac One being given by the preclear to a victim.

BEFORE EARTH

There is a BEFORE EARTH and a BEFORE MEST UNIVERSE in all banks. The incidents are not dissimilar. They consist of the preclear being summoned before a council, being frowned down, being sent elsewhere than where he was.

The odd part of these incidents to the preclear is that he is usually not guilty of anything, not aware of having offended. He is simply recruited, is brought in, is sentenced to be transported and goes to a new area.

The only thing remarkable about these Before incidents is that they are a very definite degradation and condemnation of the preclear. They are best run by scanning the preclear backwards on each column of the Chart of Attitudes from, for instance, I KNOW NOT to I KNOW, etc., for the council's intent is to reduce the person downscale in order to get a more obedient colonist.

THE JOINER

There are three major JOINERS on the track. Most of them found will be second facsimiles and do not need to be run.

Here is the basic on entities. A person is "packed in" with other souls by electronics. Actually, these entities are synthetic. Very early on the track, two more entities were "added" to the victim. They were, the three, placed in a ring and hammered by electronics to get them to fuse. There is an empty spot in the center. A later Joiner adds two more "souls." These incidents are responsible for the preclear being "softened-up" to a point where he can be influenced by having a hypnotized soul thrown at him. You will find the marks of these souls on every preclear. They are the basics on demon circuits. An entity favors the environment, not the preclear, and treats the preclear just like somebody in the environment treated the preclear. If you ask the entities questions, the areas (having demon circuits in them) will respond. If you ask the entities why they are there, they will tell you that they were the crew of the thetan, who is asleep, that they will not work, that they were all bundled together and sent here. The thetan response is that he made twelve errors, eventually could not control his crew, went into ARC with them, became like an entity, was bundled up—thetan, crew and all—and shipped down here to work matters out. The entities seem to be most interested in keeping data away from the thetan, convincing him he has done wrong. Each entity claims to have had a function that was very specialized. Insane people are found to be running on their entities, not their thetans. This is a very bad condition, betokening very solid valence walls. Every entity can be audited independently of the others. Past deaths can be run out of them with the relief of many somatics. Each has a body, so they say, in pawn elsewhere.

Here is a wealth of data and detail. Fortunately, none of it is very important to us at this time except in understanding the behavior of Homo sapiens. For these entities, regardless of auditing, work overtime on the preclear. However, in auditing the theta line, one is interested only in auditing the thetan and this is very easy to do with the incidents given above and below. One ignores the entities. They may be simply borrowed banks. They do not interfere with auditing, for their incidents all run like second facsimiles.

And although they register at first on an E-Meter, they drop out the moment the auditor asks if the incident comes from a borrowed bank. If we had to audit through the complexity and aberration of the entities, we would not have a very easy time of it. Fortunately, it is not generally necessary to even think or know about entities in order to audit the thetan. The Joiners, so far as I can establish at this time, can be ignored. If an entity pops up and won't be ignored, just make your preclear move into him and audit out where the entity is stuck on the track (psychotic) and the trouble stops.

Considerable time was spent on entities in these investigations. There was a great deal of data about them yet to learn when they were bypassed in the discovery of direct methods of auditing the thetan who, after all, *is* the preclear. A case of paralysis, however, was partially remedied by bringing the entity, who governed that side, up to present time and putting the thetan in charge of the area again. Experiment with them, for your own information, if you like. You'll find entities lie, cheat, hold out data and act generally neurotic or psychotic. Here is your "circuit case." As the thetan loses control over his environment and his body, these entities move in on areas. Rehabilitate the thetan and the entity problem vanishes. Start auditing entities and they increase in power.

These questions are at this time not answered satisfactorily: Are entities sub-beings or are they simply electronic installations? Are they very decadent thetans who have been blanketed by the preclear? Have they simply decayed until they followed the GE line? Are they control factors from between-lives? This question has been answered: Is it necessary to audit entities? And the answer to that is, No.

THE ICE CUBE

Here is an intriguing incident which, if your preclear demands, should be audited. This is evidently a method of transportation of beings to a new area. The being is packed in ice, is taken to the new area and is usually dumped in the ocean. Your preclear, if he has this one in restimulation, has very cold hands and feet chronically.

A thetan responds to hypnosis, pain, force and other factors. He also responds to being frozen in ice.

You may wonder how the being, if the ICE CUBE is used or is necessary at all, can then get into the between-lives area so easily. In other words, if he can be transported between-lives with ease, why should he be dumped originally in the form of an ice pack? Possibly the answer lies in two invader crews at work: An old invader, already in command of an area but rather downscale, controls by between-lives. A new invader crew, with more ambition, plants beings in the same area. These beings then fall into the between-lives routine which exists unbeknownst to the new crew. The new crew in the area is later quite surprised to find that their planted beings, so carefully dumped in the sea from a saucer, are being picked up between-lives and given "treatment" by an old, established invader whose methods of political control are long since established. When such a discovery is made, the new crew may very likely knock out some of the old crew installations and upset the routine.

The Ice Cube is quite authentic.

BETWEEN-LIVES

At death, the theta being leaves the body and goes to the BETWEEN-LIVES area. Here he "reports in," is given a strong forgetter implant and is then shot down to a body just before it is born. At least that is the way the old invader in the Earth area was operating.

The implant is very interesting. The preclear is seated before a wheel which contains numbers of pictures. As the wheel turns, these pictures go away from him. He is moved aside to the right, the left, the back. A mirror arrangement shows him still sitting there before the pictures. A force screen hits him through the pictures. The pictures dim out. The whole effect is to give him the impression that he has no past life, that he is no longer the same identity, that his memory has been erased. The force screen flattens his own vitality, thus invalidating his existence, thus installing, by force alone, a forgetter.

The pictures, by the way, are simply generalized views—stills of vacant lots, houses, backyards—of a recent Earth period and they could apply to anybody. They are not the facsimiles of the preclear.

The incident contains such force that the preclear, at first quite closely in contact, runs it willingly. As the force cuts down his past identity, he begins to disbelieve the incident, then himself. If left in restimulation, he has a difficult time remembering things for some days.

Gradually, through a lifetime, this Between-Lives incident keys-in. At first it engulfs childhood, then later and later years. Finally, with age, the preclear starts to cycle through it automatically and goes into a "second childhood"—which is to say, he anticipates the coming implant, conceives it to have been done if he lives beyond a normal life span for him. (If it usually happened that he died at sixty, should he now live to seventy he will get a feeling in the last ten years that it has been done to him—a routine time restimulation effect.)

Preclears do not always report. To have been implanted once is to get a restimulation on dying which will wipe out the past life. Some preclears have one, some have five, some more of these implants.

The life-to-life forgetter would follow, as a natural course of events, from the fact that the preclear identifies himself and is identified by others as a MEST body. Further, he identifies everyone else as a MEST body. Also, he would rather start, if he must be a MEST body, with a clean slate and a new body. Also, he has many overt acts of convincing others they should forget their entire pasts, for by that he can train them for a better future for him. *No* implant would *ever* succeed unless there was a natural cause and reason for the implant to magnify.

The report area for most has been Mars. Some women report to stations elsewhere in the solar system. There are occasional incidents about Earth report stations. The report stations are protected by screens. The last Martian report station on Earth was established in the Pyrenees.

Entities have Between-Lives incidents independent of the thetan. These are not necessary to run.

There are many types of Between-Lives earlier on the track, about ten different periods of the entire track being devoted to a practice of keeping a thetan in a body, working and in an area. These show up as second facsimiles and are not necessary to run. But the data is there in the secondary banks and it is very "wonderful" data on how to keep races enslaved.

THE EMANATOR

Now and then your preclear is found "stuck" in the EMANATOR. This is a large, glowing body of radioactive material which hangs magically in thin air, a sort of a god, an all-knower. Its outpulse puts one into a trance.

The story usually starts with the preclear "volunteering" to come to Earth and do good. He walks into the presence of the Emanator and that is that. He has volunteered, perhaps, simply out of curiosity, wondering what is contained in that big building. His "agreement" is, of course, enforced. He is told that they will keep his body safe for him. He "agrees" to go help out and is transported by hypnotic transference.

It never occurs to the preclear to question the safety of his body. He reports back to it Between-Lives. The body is preserved and can stay that way for some thousands of years. But bodies do not last forever. One day the preclear dies on Earth and reports back dutifully to find no body. After that he conceives himself to be lost. He is given no new goals Between-Lives, he is ignored. The next life may find him knocking on the door of a psychiatrist, for he is very "lost" and "homeless" and generally bewildered. Running the Emanator sequence and loss makes all right again.

The Emanator trick as a recruiting device is very old. You will find many second facsimiles about it in the preclear's bank.

The Double-Body

With one BODY in a trance in one place and another BODY here on Earth, trouble occasionally occurs.

A preclear during an operation may switch bodies. Pain and anesthetic or a serious accident causes him to change to the other area with a shocking impact on the other body. The other body quite commonly dies or is deranged by this sudden impact. The preclear wakes up from unconsciousness on Earth and tells (or represses) the fact that he has died. Obviously, as the surgeon or doctor will attest, he didn't die, for the heart of the patient kept beating. Actually, the patient flicked into the other body, transferred the shock and pain and killed it, then came back here and awakened.

This incident leaves a patient very, very badly disturbed. The surge into the Between-Lives area is so obviously not a death that attendants there, if attracted, will knock the body there out with commands to forget, to not let anyone know in order to "protect" the mystery. Everyone, particularly mental doctors, has in the past accounted for this circumstance (of the patient thinking he died) with wild theories about the effects of anesthetics and delusion. But no patient, so treated, ever recovered by being informed that "it is all anesthetic nightmare and delusion." And they do recover immediately if the incident is run out. Nitrous oxide is very vicious in this regard, for it does not dull any pain, it simply "drowns" the patient.

Patients wake up after such a Double-Body incident with the feeling that they have just learned the secret of the Universe, but they can't quite recall it. They have, to some extent. They've learned they're kept and implanted elsewhere.

It is important for an auditor to know that a Double-Body may have happened some lifetimes ago during an accident. To a preclear who doesn't know of the past life, much less the Double-Body, the result is quite alarming.

To run a Double-Body, run the operation or accident on Earth, then run the incident as from the other body in pawn. Then run going "under" on Earth and waking in the other body and then waking on Earth. Then run being in the other place and appearing on Earth.

Run the Double-Body until it is very thoroughly reduced, running the overt acts on it as well, which will be what the preclear says they are.

THETA TRAPS

There is no subject more interesting than that of THETA TRAPS. It is of vast interest to any invader. It is of vaster interest to your preclear. How can you trap a thetan? By curiosity, by giving him awards and prizes (of an implant), by retractor screens, by mock-ups, by ornate buildings which he will enter unsuspectingly only to be "electroniced down," by many such means the thetan is reduced from KNOWING to a colonist, a slave, a MEST body.

All theta traps have one thing in common: They use electronic force to knock the thetan into forgetting, into unknowingness, into effect. Their purpose is to rid the area of those nuisances, the thetans who cannot be policed, and to gain personnel—always the former, not always the latter.

The thetan feels himself, in some traps, being drawn up to a post. He fights it with his force. It cannot be successfully fought. He succumbs. A day or a hundred years later, he is picked off and elsewise used.

A thetan can sustain many implants of this character without becoming obsessed about having a body. But he becomes obsessed very easily about having facsimiles.

The Jack-in-the-Box is a variety of theta trap.

After he was caught in some kind of theta trap, the thetan was handled as follows:

The Body Builder

Sometimes a thetan is taken off a theta trap and put into a field which makes him fight again with his attention units. The purpose of this field is to make him resist its force and to resist it so as to mold him. Out of his attention units he "builds" a body. Later he is given sharp shots through the places where joints are supposed to be and is generally tailored into a body. There were many of these on the whole track. In your preclear, they are probably second facsimiles.

The Body Builder used some fifty million years ago was very precise. Although it has degenerated and is less formalized and although it is doubtful if you will find it in more than a second facsimile, the original version is given here.

The Jiggler

Placed over a post, the thetan was moved up and down rapidly and eccentrically for some time. He would try to hold on to and stop the post, would go into apathy and finish by being entirely invalidated as himself and would think of himself as the post—that having become cause.

The Whirler

The thetan was placed on a platform which whirled eccentrically, jerkily, to the left and right until he would turn as the post turned.

The Bouncer

The thetan was bounced up and down eccentrically until he had a facsimile which fixed him, it would appear, on his time track.

The Spinner

A chair device was used to spin the thetan until he had no orientation. This is the probable source of the slang term "spinning"—meaning, going insane.

THE ROCKER

This swung or teetered the thetan to the left and right, slowly and quietly.

This incident is dramatized today by mystics who, not being quite low enough on the scale to die, finish the job by picking up old electronic implant motions and practice them until they have "control of the body"—which they mean to mean, without meaning to mean it, complete body control of "I".

THE BOXER

This incident is a cousin to the "Fly-Trap."

Its purpose was to make the thetan into a complete stimulus-response mechanism. He was hit from every angle by a device not unlike a boxing glove. He would be forced to kick back against it with his force. At length, he would be psychotic enough to return every motion he received.

This is actually aberration itself. It is the psychologist's definition, though vaguely put, of a "well-adjusted human being"—one who stimulates and responds without thought.

THE FALLER

This installs a fear of falling, also fixes the thetan in the incident on the track. He is dropped again and again and again to different drops and at varied intervals until he is jammed.

THE EDUCATION

After all these, the thetan was given a complete education.

This was of a hypnotic, stimulus-response variety. It was the type of education which makes a file-card system out of a thinking being. It is dramatized today in universities as it requires no skilled instruction.

The Fly-Trap

Very, very early on the track, a long time before any of the present populace came into being, there was a theta trap called the Fly-Trap. It was of a gummy material. The thetan who got into it punched and fought at this material until he was psychotic enough to react to the physical universe laws of responding to motions. He was taken out of this trap by a crew of do-gooders who had caught him "for his own good" and who trained him in religious sweetness and syrup until they considered him fit to be part of their group. The attitude of these people was *so* good, their manners *so* understanding, that the thetan usually ran away as soon as possible.

Sunday school sometimes brings this, even as a second facsimile which it nearly always is, into heavy restimulation.

Remember, auditor, that a second facsimile doesn't have to be audited, but will blow when the preclear sees that he "borrowed" it from somebody. But that doesn't mean he won't use it. Lacking a motivator, your preclear, guilty of some overt act, will go back into his "borrowings" and pick out any second facsimile which looks vicious enough to justify his own action. And he will use it to the hilt. Thus, you may find your preclear stuck in incidents of great age and fury. You may find him with Arsclycus in full bloom (where they spent ten thousand lives laboring on the same job, were stuffed like snakes every few weeks to feed them, where they returned after death because a piece of their own body was held in pawn) and unable to work and given to a weariness beyond description. Located as a second facsimile, the entire incident tends to depart. Or, locating the overt act the preclear actually did himself, the second facsimile goes without auditing.

If a preclear holds hard to a second facsimile, he is guilty of more overt acts than he is telling the auditor or the incident is something else than it appears to be.

Ask your E-Meter.

GENERALIZED

"A DED is an incident the preclear does to another dynamic and for which he has no motivator."

Ten

INCIDENTS

Chapter Ten

GENERALIZED INCIDENTS

ENERALIZED INCIDENTS would include anything the preclear has done which is an opposite motion to the incident in which he is "hung-up." The opposite motion is what hangs the incident up.

MOTIVATOR

A MOTIVATOR is an incident which happens to the preclear and which he dramatizes.

OVERT ACT

An OVERT ACT (which may also be covert or accidental) is an incident which the preclear does to another dynamic.

DED

A DED is an incident the preclear does to another dynamic and for which he has no motivator—i.e., he punishes or hurts or wrecks something the like of which has never hurt him. Now he must justify the incident. He will use things which didn't happen to him. He claims that the object of his injury really deserved it, hence the word, which is a sarcasm.

Dedex

A DEDEX is an incident which happens to a preclear *after* he has a DED. It is always on the same chain or subject, is always after the DED. It means the DED EXPOSED. It is covered guilt. Its effect on the preclear is all out of proportion to the actual injury to him. One would think he was murdered by the harsh word or the scratch. He will explain violently how terribly he has been used. Whenever you have a preclear who has been too abused for words and keeps on giving you incidents which tend to fix the guilt on the family or women or some such thing, the auditor can recognize in these DEDEXes and know that he must look for the DED. The preclear is usually quite unwilling to give up the DED, but the E-Meter will find it. It is on the same subject as the DEDEXes: If he has many incidents about things his mother did to him and these seem fairly routine, there is a previous incident about his mother or some earlier-life mother where, with an unmotivated cruelty, he executed a DED.

Misassist

A MISASSIST is an incident wherein the preclear has tried to help on some dynamic and failed. These are very aberrative. The incident may be short and harsh or it may be a large number of small incidents. The MISASSIST is a failure to assist either by omission or commission. It is always preceded by a MOTIVATOR–OVERT situation lock-up or a DED–DEDEX situation. The preclear, having injured some dynamic, has come into the state of protecting that dynamic out of all proportion to the other dynamics. Perhaps he has many times succeeded in his protection and such incidents are not aberrative. But one day he tries to assist and fails, or he should have assisted and didn't, and the result is the "straw" added to the weight of an earlier facsimile hang-up.

Degrader

A DEGRADER is an incident or chain of incidents whereby a low-toned person seeks to bring down the tone of a higher-toned person. The actual intent of the low-toned person is to get another low enough so that the latter can be helped. The low-toned person believes he cannot be of assistance to anything higher on the scale than himself. Therefore he will attempt to reduce the tone of another and then, when he has him well down by degrading him, he will be able to assist, becomes sympathetic and conducts himself properly until, of course, the person is up again. The preclear will, if very low-toned, try this on the auditor. Any low-toned person will do it. The preclear may have many degraders he has done. Or he may have had many degraders happen to him. If the preclear is prone to degraders, he has a DED–DEDEX situation on the same dynamic he permits to degrade him: If he accepts criticism from women, he has a DED–DEDEX on women. If he claims it was father who got him down, who invalidated him, he has a DED–DEDEX on his own father or some past father or man who looks like his father. If you find a degrader situation, look for the DED–DEDEX on the same subject. If the preclear is given to invalidating, he has a degrader chain he has done. The dynamic he degrades has a prior DED–DEDEX.

THE

"A thetan is pretty bad off
 if he thinks all he can do is
  run a MEST body."

TRANSFER

Chapter Eleven

THE TRANSFER

*T*HE TRANSFER is the single most important phase of Technique 88. It is a circumstance rather than an incident. It is a specific action of the thetan with regard to a MEST body. It is the swing of the thetan from out of the body, where he belongs, into the body, where he is thereafter in trouble.

The TRANSFER is the action of going into the MEST body.

Except in deaths or severe accidents or operations, you won't find a Transfer out. Your task in auditing is to find and run all the Transfers into bodies in order to achieve a self-determined, fully alive Transfer out.

WHERE is the thetan? Contrary to any past practice, his second-best place is just outside the MEST body, monitoring it with direct contact on the MEST body's motor controls on either side of the head. His very best place, of course, is out of contact with the MEST body entirely and fully alive as "I". His worst place is inside the MEST body.

The thetan, in most cases, is behind and above the MEST body. In many cases he shifts position rather often, even in one incident. Now and then he is found to run the body from in front of it. This causes a direction reversal on the part of the person so that he doesn't know right from left. People can teach him continually, but he will still say his right is his left and his left is his right. And so it is. For "I" in this person is the thetan and the thetan is in front—facing the MEST body—and right is the thetan's right, of course.

There are cases where the thetan is barely or hardly ever in contact with the body. These cases can be considered quite aberrated, the thetan seeing the body from across rooms or streets, convinced that he is the body, but unable to do anything about it. There are cases where the thetan is inside the body continually. But this is to say that he isn't a thetan at all, but degenerated into an entity—and we find this in those low-tone, wide-open cases, full on but raving psychotics or nearly so.

A thetan is pretty bad off if he thinks all he can do is run a MEST body. This alone is a HALF-TRANSFER. He hasn't gone into the body yet, forever thereafter perhaps to be an entity. But he has achieved the level of degradation where he thinks the MEST body is more important than he is and that he *is* the MEST body. He has become propitiative toward the body to a point where he is a servant, where it becomes him in his eyes.

A FULL TRANSFER occurs many times in the span of a thetan. But it is not permanent until he enters the body to stay in there from there on.

In doing a DED, a thetan catches the sorrow waves of the body he is wronging, feels sorry for it and then, for one reason or another, merges into it. This is a TEMPORARY TRANSFER. But after a few of these, he will become obsessed with being the monitor of a MEST body and will devote all his time to it. Then he will suppose that his only method of perceiving is through MEST perceptics, his only method of emoting is through MEST emotions. And he comes way on down the scale, becomes a servant, feels so degraded that he is himself nothing and the MEST body everything and so tends it continually. Eventually, he will merge with it in a PERMANENT TRANSFER and that is probably the end of the thetan—the genetic entity and company thereafter perhaps running from within, perhaps in the next life being picked up by a new thetan. Thetans are continually being pumped into the MEST line. They do not last very long. The "I" of the individual is the thetan.

The foregoing paragraph contains steps which the auditor must know. This is the cycle he is trying to work out of the case.

You will find many conditions occurring in the Transfer. There is another type of Transfer, the SWITCH TRANSFER, wherein a thetan, to protect the body he has assumed, changes in sudden moments his control to a person startling or attacking the thetan's property. This can become very bad and very involved. It happens in families and amongst friends and when they part or somebody dies, the thetan is suddenly bereft of some of the property he was controlling and so carries on as if MEST was important.

The CONTROL TRANSFER is a specialized kind of Transfer, wherein the thetan, having devoted himself to a MEST body, now begins to control the environment and other people for his body, much as he controls the body. Having forgotten his skills and having many brands of aberration, whereby he will Transfer permanently at least some of his control, he yet adventures to reach out energy-wise and start to control other people than his own body and also attempt to control MEST objects and motions. He is at first very capable in this but, having aberrations which cause him to stick on things, his control of the environment becomes too extended. When he loses some of the environment, he conceives that he has lost some of his ability to control. We get, then, a dwindling of control along all the dynamics throughout the lifetime until he finally cannot even control all the MEST body, but only some small part of it. A thetan without aberration could safely enter into and control the whole environment, lose widely and reassume control. A thetan very aberrated will get restimulated when he loses some control of the environment and won't thereafter try to control that type of thing or person again. These Control Transfers and their losses will be found widely in any case and are almost as important as auditing control of the First Dynamic.

As you run facsimiles, you will find that there are those seen by the preclear as though within himself and those seen by the preclear as though outside himself. Audit the latter to audit the thetan. Audit the former and you audit only entities.

CONFUSION OF IDENTITY is a primary problem with preclears. Now that WHO the preclear is can be established and WHERE he is can be seen by the preclear as he runs facsimiles, this confusion can be resolved. But do not expect to solve it for the preclear rapidly. And do not expect to be right yourself the first time.

Technique 88 is an E-Meter technique. It can be run without an E-Meter, but this permits all manner of dodging and evading. And there are usually six or ten entirely different banks in any preclear besides his own—lots of places to dodge into.

The entities all have banks. Now these are either stolen banks (from some other thetan long ago, as in Borrowing) or they are the identity of this entity. We aren't much interested in auditing entities except when auditing one can reduce rapidly a physical somatic or physical ill—easily done, for the entities hold these in present time and they will audit in present time. A thetan high enough to be outside the body to a normal control distance is not going to hold a facsimile in restimulation just to hurt or injure his body. Only an entity will do this or a thetan who has Transferred all the way into the body—which makes him an entity and thereafter he will behave like one (no work, high ARC with groups in order to upset them covertly, etc., etc.).

You will find an understanding of your thetan's goals a little helpful in making sure you are auditing the thetan. He was quite old when he first fixated on the idea of controlling MEST bodies. That was not too long ago if he is still operating just outside the body (about arm's length). One of the reasons he fixated on a MEST body was because he was terribly bored.

There is a considerable liability to being a thetan from the standpoint that one is quite immortal. Even death cycles will look good to a thetan whose aberrations have reduced him down from the goals and hopes he once had. Now he begins to have hopes for a MEST body. This body will grow and die, but at least it will change. Aberrations cut this thetan down to a point where he couldn't see any change possible, could not see his own goals would ever be attained. So he fixated on a MEST body, became involved in the pure mechanics of operating and caring for one, became more aberrated by contagion from the entities in that body and the uncertainty of life in a mortal being, lost his goals as a MEST body and, finally, became pretty sordidly sick of the whole thing.

Now, magically, you uncover for this thetan six or eight banks full of 70 trillion years or less of incident. The thetan is a wizard at liking to act at being somebody else. That got him into believing he himself was a MEST body. Well, it will also get him into believing he is any one of the entity banks you uncover. And he will let you audit these things until doomsday. Vicarious existence, better than a motion picture.

But ask this thetan to confront the existence which he shudderingly forsook? Never! It was boring. He's been through all that. He actually knows what happened to him, but it was bad enough to make him wish to forget it—until he forgot it. He'll say he's this entity or that. He'll be happy, in preference to facing his own past, to just go on and perish as a MEST body.

There are two remedies for this.

The first is the E-Meter. That is an unequaled remedy. You can find out the identity of every bank in the preclear and know that the thetan isn't any of them. You can find out the first to last Transfers. You can discover the location of every incident the thetan should run.

Now, in using the E-Meter, you will discover something strange with regard to the thetan. At first, the meter will be much more active on the entities than on the thetan himself. For one thing, the thetan is *outside* the body. For another, the thetan would rather look over and shove into view incidents he himself has never before seen. He'll help you audit those entities endlessly.

People who keep running incidents without any recourse to an E-Meter will achieve much with the body, very little with the thetan. Hence, there is no rise in tone although the auditing hours continue to stretch out.

In people who continually self-audit without direction, the thetan is just being very propitiative toward MEST bodies and is giving the entities a wonderful workout. The body gets better sometimes. The thetan never gets better. And he is "I".

The behavior of the thetan in the past was often copied after something he took from the entities. He found an entity role would restimulate, he became the actor and performed the role. He left his own bank alone and neglected, although there were aberrations to dramatize there too. (And by the way, you will find the thetan occasionally trying to stop the body from dramatizing out of entity banks.)

The thetan bank, the one you want, will give you less active needle response than the entity banks when you first start auditing. This is a sort of negative sorting. But you may have to audit an entity or two because of the way the entity has the body stuck on the track.

The point is to find the thetan bank and audit it. The conflict in this person derives from the ambitions of the thetan being balked by the laziness and stupidity and desire for death and destruction on the part of the entities. You can audit any side of this conflict you want. But by simply making the thetan sufficiently strong, the entities become cowed and won't act up, or even drop out and leave.

The other answer is to clean up present life with attention to all Transfers in it, all Switch Transfers, all Control Transfers. Audit the thetan handling the body until you have the current life well up. This does not take very long with Technique 80.

You will find that you will have to start by giving the preclear a drill to locate where the thetan is. Simply run him up and down the track through various incidents, with good attention to Attention Unit Running, each time locating the thetan outside the body and handling it. The preclear will get a dim concept of the handling, but he will get a good concept of the location of the thetan. Now, in the current lifetime, locate the thetan being distracted from his task by noises or arguments in the environment.

Run the sympathy of the thetan for the body, the refusal of the thetan to feel sympathy at times. And run, in particular, antagonisms or angers from the body at other bodies, from the other bodies at the thetan's body. Get all the DED–DEDEX computations out of the way and then audit the thetan entrance somewhere around the time of birth. It isn't an entrance, it's a possession of the motor controls.

When you have this thetan in good shape for this lifetime, he will be strong enough, usually, to tackle Nips, Blanketings, Borrowings. But don't be amazed, when you run your first of these, to find that the thetan has been using an entity bank. Any Borrowing, however, is good to run. Any Blanketing on the Second Dynamic shows your preclear once and for all that he *is* a theta being without a body, by showing him an incident to that effect.

If the case is incapable of finding the thetan in current life, then take the youngest entity and audit it. It generally is the thetan, but Transferred inside the body.

How long it will take you to audit a preclear to Theta Clear, one cannot say. The route reaches high very quickly. Using this know-how and 80, you will attain a MEST Clear in a very short time. Aside from inaccessible persons and psychotics in general, most cases should become MEST Clear in a few weeks of hard auditing.

A
STEP-BY-STEP

"The thetan's aberration
toward the body is to want things
to seem real to the thetan
via the body."

BREAKDOWN OF 88

A Step-by-Step Breakdown of 88

SUGGESTED ROUTINE:

SYMBOLOGICAL PROCESSING ON CURRENT LIFE UNTIL PRECLEAR IS WELL IN PRESENT TIME.

RETURN PRECLEAR TO INCIDENTS WHERE THE THETAN CAN BE LOCATED AS OUTSIDE AND IN GOOD CONTROL OF THE BODY AND RUN SUCH INCIDENTS TO ORIENT PRECLEAR.

IN ABSENCE OF AN OUTSIDE THETAN, AUDIT PRECLEAR THROUGH FAILURES TO CONTROL SELF. USE AN E-METER TO LOCATE YOUNGEST ENTITY (NEWEST BANK IN THE BODY) AND AUDIT ITS EFFORT TO CONTROL BODY. THEN AUDIT ANY TRANSFER YOU CAN FIND. THEN AUDIT BLANKETINGS UNTIL PRECLEAR FINDS THETAN IS WITHOUT A BODY.

WHERE THETAN IS OUTSIDE WHERE HE BELONGS, AUDIT PRECLEAR IN CURRENT LIFE THROUGH ANY AND ALL DEDs AND DEDEXes AND DEGRADERS.

AUDIT ALL PRESENT LIFE TRANSFERS OF THE THETAN, ALL SWITCH AND CONTROL TRANSFERS THAT CAN BE FOUND.

RUN OFF ALL INCIDENTS IN PRESENT LIFE WHERE THETAN AND BODY CREATE BOIL-OFF. (DON'T BE SURPRISED AT THETAN VISIOS. YOU'RE AUDITING THETA, NOT MEST PERCEPTION.)

137

In-scan and Out-scan thetan through present life. This makes MEST Clear.

With E-Meter, locate first implant about having facsimiles in thetan. Audit it.

Locate first Borrowings. Audit them.

Locate first Blanketings. Audit them.

Locate DEDs and DEDEXes of thetan and audit them.

Locate each and every Transfer on track. Audit them.

The thetan concentrates on the body. He is usually about arm's length from the body, concentrating on the body. When he is not concentrating on the body, there is a disturbance in the area and the thetan is being distracted to another body or object. These distractions are important to audit.

Don't ask your preclear to get any other visio on the scene than the visio of the body the thetan is manipulating. This is the usual thetan position and only interest.

Don't be dissuaded that the preclear is not the thetan. That he thinks he is not is the aberration.

The most fixative emotions are resentment, antagonism and anger. These tend to fix the thetan on the body. They confirm a Transfer as permanent.

The thetan's aberration toward the body is to want things to seem real to the thetan via the body. Actually, the thetan should feel at least a little remote and detached as though he weren't quite present. This detachment will increase as auditing continues to the great benefit of the intelligence and ability.

THE PRECLEAR GETS BETTER THE BETTER THE THETAN GETS
AND THAT IS ALL THE BETTER THE PRECLEAR CAN GET.

ADDITIONAL

INCIDENTS

"*Peculiarly aberrative are
Theta Trap Posts. This is
the basic of one having
a body.*"

ON THE
THETA LINE

August 1952

Supplement

ADDITIONAL INCIDENTS ON THE THETA LINE *

GLARE FIGHTS

Early on the track, two thetans quite often went into contest with each other to GLARE each other down. There was a considerable output of electrical energy and in the interchange one of the thetans was, of course, driven into apathy.

These incidents are audited simply by following the flow of energy and collecting out of it its beauty and ugliness and the preclear's agreement, disagreement, communication, no-communication, affinity and unaffinity for the beauty and ugliness contained in these flows.

MIRRORS

A common protection used by beings against thetans was a MIRROR. The thetan would send a stream of energy at the being carrying the mirror and the stream of energy would, of course, be directed straight back at the thetan so he would be in the strange position of glaring at himself.

* This supplement of *Additional Incidents* includes discoveries subsequent to initial publication of *History of Man* and contains further breakthroughs and technology as described in the book *Scientology 8-80*. —Editor

EXPLODING FACSIMILES

In Blanketings, one of the most serious points is the fact that death facsimiles can EXPLODE. Death shock is well known to produce a heavy electronic output from beings. This output can be so sudden that any facsimiles suspended in present time are fed so many attention units so quickly that the facsimile can be said to explode. A person being Blanketed, if he dies, feeds out a considerable electronic shock which explodes those facsimiles he has in suspension. The thetan, Blanketing him, starts to get off, feels the expansion of the shock, clamps down on the being and completes, one might say, the demolition of the facsimiles by adding additional energy into them. This is quite severe and leaves an individual holding a Blanketing in fear because of this explosion. People who have anxiety stomachs lose them very rapidly when one runs out Blanketings and the explosions of the facsimiles.

IMPLOSIONS

A thetan, or any energy, can IMPLODE as well as EXPLODE. This is the effect of a retractor factor present in electrical energy. Instead of exploding and blowing out into a larger sphere, the energy implodes and draws into a much smaller area with the same suddenness that it would explode.

To run this, it is only necessary to put one's attention on the center of the implosion and then, alternately, get the effort to draw off from the sphere of implosion. Putting one's attention on the center and then trying to draw off, and on the center and trying to draw off again, will run out an implosion.

THE CAPPER

This is a very early incident on the track and consists of a thetan being crowned with an electronic CAP through which energy pours. It is an initial effort to make him have facsimiles and to derange his self-determinism.

The Prover

Here one has a thetan approaching a group of thetans. The group demands that the new thetan PROVE something. The moment he starts to prove it, the whole group invalidates him. This causes him to go rapidly down the Tone Scale in an effort to prove that he knows. He then may become part of the group and in playing this game on other new thetans who approach, eventually may become at odds with the group and be rejected from the group.

The Prover is located by getting the beauty or ugliness of trying to prove something to somebody and others trying to prove things to oneself.

The Iron Maiden

This is a relatively recent incident, happening only two thousand or three thousand years ago. It consists of a shell, not unlike THE IRON MAIDEN used in the Middle Ages. The thetan is pulled into this shell and it is closed on him. He furnishes the bulk of energy in the shell—the shell is highly magnetic and extra energy is fed to it. On the right half, one ordinarily gets a vertical flow. Simultaneously, on the left half, one ordinarily gets horizontal flow. These two flows, going on in different directions at the same time, can cause considerable confusion and are the basic reasons why the left sides and right sides will not run out at the same time.

This incident is quite hidden on the E-Meter, showing up simply as a stuck needle. The entire motive of this incident is hiding—fear of discovery, shrinking into oneself and so forth, as an effort to get away from the confusing flows of the shell itself. It is run, as to locks, by hiding things from others and others hiding things from self.

There are sexual and religious connotations in this incident. It also seems to divide a person into male and female gender, one on the left and one on the right, and makes one think he must be dual to survive. This is also found as a factor in other incidents.

Theta Trap Posts

Peculiarly aberrative are THETA TRAP POSTS. This is the basic of one having a body. It ordinarily happened very early on the track. A single post is set up, sometimes in a cave or in a place a thetan might have been known to inhabit. The post itself has no electrical current in it. All electrical current in this incident is furnished by the thetan himself. The post is simply a large magnet. The thetan, when he first senses this post, feels it drawing him toward it. This is because of his own electrical energy. He fights back against this post and the harder he fights the post, the closer he comes to it, until at last he blankets the post. Probably this method of trapping thetans was invented out of rancor for the activity of thetans in Blanketing and a magnet is given the thetan to blanket. Thereafter, every time any energy flows through this thetan on the post, the post picks up the energy and flows it back up inside him. Other beings of a lower order may come up and discharge weapons at him or antagonize him so that he will throw a current out at them. Each time he does, he gets the current himself. This is probably a basic on the overt act phenomenon and, at least, exaggerates it. Thetans have spent anything from five days up to a hundred years on such posts before being taken off them. The thetan eventually learns to control his output and input in such a way as not to use any electrical energy. Later, when he gets on a body, this incident may go into restimulation and thereafter he is afraid to get angry at anyone. And when he does, he feels the kickback of the facsimile against himself. This is a relatively simple incident to run, particularly with beauty and ugliness in all the flows, but it is rather long.

The Parity

There is an early incident on the track called THE PARITY. A thetan is made to sit opposite an image like himself and a metallic beam (or, actually, a piece of metal) is put in his mouth and in the mouth of the being opposite him. Any activity thereafter causes an interchange of energy and confirms the overt act phenomenon. This is peculiarly restimulated by marriage.

AUDITING

In auditing, one audits, according to 8-80,* the high aesthetic wave only. This is present in every incident to a marked degree—the white representing beauty, the black representing ugliness. The Iron Maiden is an exception to this. The Iron Maiden flows gray rapidly as the thetan withdraws into himself so tightly. Therefore, only a gray is present afterwards.

Assignment of responsibility in any incident is the most important factor in the incident, since this assignment of responsibility to somebody else for causing the incident puts the incident itself out of the control of the person having the facsimile. As a person assigns responsibility to others, he assigns at the same time to them the control for his facsimiles. Thus he loses control of the facsimiles, claims he does not own them, loses all memory in connection with them and they can thereafter own and run him.

The whole sequence of aberration is at first being self-determined, then being hit hard enough by force to have a new determination entered into one which is not his, but which he would use thereafter as his own. This gradual shift and change of determination, other than one's own determination, brings about a highly aberrated condition in the long run and makes it difficult for a person to sort out where he is actually caught.

In order to get a preclear off a body, or to detach him from bodies, Technique 8-80 is used with particular attention to the assignment of responsibility. For the preclear has assigned responsibility to the body so long and so often, has assigned responsibility to bodies in general to such a degree, that he thinks that he himself is nothing. When the body dies, he thinks memories die of that body, which is not the case. This is the occlusion on the past.

---

* See the book *Scientology 8-80*.

A P P E N D I X

FURTHER STUDY

BOOKS & LECTURES BY L. RON HUBBARD

The materials of Dianetics and Scientology comprise the largest body of information ever assembled on the mind, spirit and life, rigorously refined and codified by L. Ron Hubbard through five decades of research, investigation and development. The results of that work are contained in hundreds of books and more than 3,000 recorded lectures. A full listing and description of them all can be obtained from any Scientology Church or Publications Organization. (See *Guide to the Materials*.)

The books and lectures below form the foundation upon which the Bridge to Freedom is built. They are listed in the sequence Ron wrote or delivered them. In many instances, Ron gave a series of lectures immediately following the release of a new book to provide further explanation and insight of these milestones. Through monumental restoration efforts, those lectures are now available and are listed herein with their companion book.

While Ron's books contain the summaries of breakthroughs and conclusions as they appeared in the developmental research track, his lectures provide the running day-to-day record of research and explain the thoughts, conclusions, tests and demonstrations that lay along that route. In that regard, they are the complete record of the entire research track, providing not only the most important breakthroughs in Man's history, but the *why* and *how* Ron arrived at them.

Not the least advantage of a chronological study of these books and lectures is the inclusion of words and terms which, when originally used, were defined by LRH with considerable exactitude. Far beyond a mere "definition," entire lectures are devoted to a full description of each new Dianetic or Scientology term—what made the breakthrough possible, its application in auditing as well as its application to life itself. As a result, one leaves behind no misunderstoods, obtains a full conceptual understanding of Dianetics and Scientology and grasps the subjects at a level not otherwise possible.

Through a sequential study, you can see how the subject progressed and recognize the highest levels of development. The listing of books and lectures below shows where *Scientology: A History of Man* fits within the developmental line. From there you can determine your *next* step or any earlier books and lectures you may have missed. You will then be able to fill in missing gaps, not only gaining knowledge of each breakthrough, but greater understanding of what you've already studied.

This is the path to knowing how to know, unlocking the gates to your future eternity. Follow it.

DIANETICS: THE ORIGINAL THESIS • Ron's *first* description of Dianetics. Originally circulated in manuscript form, it was soon copied and passed from hand to hand. Ensuing word of mouth created such demand for more information, Ron concluded the only way to answer the inquiries was with a book. That book was Dianetics: The Modern Science of Mental Health, now the all-time self-help bestseller. Find out what started it all. For here is the bedrock foundation of Dianetic discoveries: the *Original Axioms,* the *Dynamic Principle of Existence,* the *Anatomy of the Analytical* and *Reactive Mind,* the *Dynamics,* the *Tone Scale,* the *Auditor's Code* and the first description of a *Clear.* Even more than that, here are the primary laws describing *how* and *why* auditing works. It's only here in Dianetics: The Original Thesis.

DIANETICS: THE EVOLUTION OF A SCIENCE • This is the story of *how* Ron discovered the reactive mind and developed the procedures to get rid of it. Originally written for a national magazine—published to coincide with the release of Dianetics: The Modern Science of Mental Health—it started a wildfire movement virtually overnight upon that book's publication. Here then are both the fundamentals of Dianetics as well as the only account of Ron's two-decade journey of discovery and how he applied a scientific methodology to the problems of the human mind. He wrote it so you would know. Hence, this book is a must for every Dianeticist and Scientologist.

DIANETICS: THE MODERN SCIENCE OF MENTAL HEALTH • The bolt from the blue that began a worldwide movement. For while Ron had previously announced his discovery of the reactive mind, it had only fueled the fire of those wanting more information. More to the point—it was humanly impossible for one man to clear an entire planet. Encompassing all his previous discoveries and case histories of those breakthroughs in application, Ron provided the complete handbook of Dianetics procedure to train auditors to use it everywhere. A bestseller for more than half a century and with tens of millions of copies in print, Dianetics: The Modern Science of Mental Health has been translated in more than fifty languages, and used in more than 100 countries of Earth—indisputably, the most widely read and influential book about the human mind ever written. And that is why it will forever be known as *Book One.*

> **DIANETICS LECTURES AND DEMONSTRATIONS** • Immediately following the publication of *Dianetics,* LRH began lecturing to packed auditoriums across America. Although addressing thousands at a time, demand continued to grow. To meet that demand, his presentation in Oakland, California, was recorded. In these four lectures, Ron related the events that sparked his investigation and his personal journey to his groundbreaking discoveries. He followed it all with a personal demonstration of Dianetics auditing—the only such demonstration of Book One available. *4 lectures.*

DIANETICS PROFESSIONAL COURSE LECTURES—*A SPECIAL COURSE FOR BOOK ONE AUDITORS* • Following six months of coast-to-coast travel, lecturing to the first Dianeticists, Ron assembled auditors in Los Angeles for a new Professional Course. The subject was his next sweeping discovery on life—the *ARC Triangle,* describing the interrelationship of *Affinity, Reality* and *Communication.* Through a series of fifteen lectures, LRH announced many firsts, including the *Spectrum of Logic,* containing an infinity of gradients from right to wrong; *ARC and the Dynamics;* the *Tone Scales of ARC;* the *Auditor's Code* and how it relates to ARC; and the *Accessibility Chart* that classifies a case and how to process it. Here, then, is both the final statement on Book One Auditing Procedures and the discovery upon which all further research would advance. The data in these lectures was thought to be lost for over fifty years and only available in student notes published in Notes on the Lectures. The original recordings have now been discovered making them broadly available for the first time. Life in its highest state, *Understanding,* is composed of Affinity, Reality and Communication. And, as LRH said, the best description of the ARC Triangle to be found anywhere is in these lectures. *15 lectures.*

SCIENCE OF SURVIVAL—*PREDICTION OF HUMAN BEHAVIOR* • The most useful book you will ever own. Built around the *Hubbard Chart of Human Evaluation,* Science of Survival provides the first accurate prediction of human behavior. Included on the chart are all the manifestations of an individual's survival potential graduated from highest to lowest, making this the complete book on the Tone Scale. Knowing only one or two characteristics of a person and using this chart, you can plot his or her position on the Tone Scale and thereby know the rest, obtaining an accurate index of their *entire* personality, conduct and character. Before this book the world was convinced that cases could not improve but only deteriorate. Science of Survival presents the idea of different states of case and the brand-new idea that one can progress upward on the Tone Scale. And therein lies the basis of today's Grade Chart.

THE SCIENCE OF SURVIVAL LECTURES • Underlying the development of the Tone Scale and Chart of Human Evaluation was a monumental breakthrough: The *Theta–MEST Theory,* containing the explanation of the interaction between Life—*theta*—with the physical universe of Matter, Energy, Space and Time—*MEST.* In these lectures, delivered to students immediately following publication of the book, Ron gave the most expansive description of all that lies behind the Chart of Human Evaluation and its application in life itself. Moreover, here also is the explanation of how the ratio of *theta* and *en(turbulated)-theta* determines one's position on the Tone Scale and the means to ascend to higher states. *4 lectures.*

SELF ANALYSIS • The barriers of life are really just shadows. Learn to know yourself—not just a shadow of yourself. Containing the most complete description of consciousness, Self Analysis takes you through your past, through your potentials, your life. First, with a series of self-examinations and using a special version of the Hubbard Chart of Human Evaluation, you plot yourself on the Tone Scale. Then, applying a series of light yet powerful processes, you embark on the great adventure of self-discovery. This book further contains embracive principles that reach *any* case, from the lowest to the highest—including auditing techniques so effective they are referred to by Ron again and again through all following years of research into the highest states. In sum, this book not only moves one up the Tone Scale but can pull a person out of almost anything.

ADVANCED PROCEDURE AND AXIOMS • With new breakthroughs on the nature and anatomy of engrams—"Engrams are effective only when the individual himself determines that they will be effective"—came the discovery of the being's use of a *Service Facsimile:* a mechanism employed to explain away failures in life, but which then locks a person into detrimental patterns of behavior and further failure. In consequence came a new type of processing addressing *Thought, Emotion* and *Effort* detailed in the "Fifteen Acts" of Advanced Procedure and oriented to the rehabilitation of the preclear's *Self-determinism.* Hence, this book also contains the all-encompassing, no-excuses-allowed explanation of *Full Responsibility,* the key to unlocking it all. Moreover, here is the codification of *Definitions, Logics,* and *Axioms,* providing both the summation of the entire subject and direction for all future research. *See Handbook for Preclears, written as a companion self-processing manual to Advanced Procedure and Axioms.*

> **THOUGHT, EMOTION AND EFFORT** • With the codification of the Axioms came the means to address key points on a case that could unravel all aberration. *Basic Postulates, Prime Thought, Cause and Effect* and their effect on everything from *memory* and *responsibility* to an individual's own role in empowering *engrams*—these matters are only addressed in this series. Here, too, is the most complete description of the *Service Facsimile* found anywhere—and why its resolution removes an individual's self-imposed disabilities. *21 lectures.*

154

HANDBOOK FOR PRECLEARS • The "Fifteen Acts" of Advanced Procedure and Axioms are paralleled by the fifteen Self-processing Acts given in Handbook for Preclears. Moreover, this book contains several essays giving the most expansive description of the *Ideal State of Man*. Discover why behavior patterns become so solidly fixed; why habits seemingly can't be broken; how decisions long ago have more power over a person than his decisions today; and why a person keeps past negative experiences in the present. It's all clearly laid out on the Chart of Attitudes—a milestone breakthrough that complements the Chart of Human Evaluation—plotting the ideal state of being and one's *attitudes* and *reactions* to life. *In self-processing, Handbook for Preclears is used in conjunction with Self Analysis.*

THE LIFE CONTINUUM • Besieged with requests for lectures on his latest breakthroughs, Ron replied with everything they wanted and more at the Second Annual Conference of Dianetic Auditors. Describing the technology that lies behind the self-processing steps of the *Handbook*—here is the *how* and *why* of it all: the discovery of *Life Continuum*—the mechanism by which an individual is compelled to carry on the life of another deceased or departed individual, generating in his own body the infirmities and mannerisms of the departed. Combined with auditor instruction on use of the Chart of Attitudes in determining how to enter every case at the proper gradient, here, too, are directions for dissemination of the Handbook and hence, the means to begin wide-scale clearing. *10 lectures.*

SCIENTOLOGY: MILESTONE ONE • Ron began the first lecture in this series with six words that would change the world forever: "This is a course in *Scientology*." From there, Ron not only described the vast scope of this, a then brand-new subject, he also detailed his discoveries on past lives. He proceeded from there to the description of the first E-Meter and its initial use in uncovering the *theta line* (the entire track of a thetan's existence), as entirely distinct from the *genetic body line* (the time track of bodies and their physical evolution), shattering the "one-life" lie and revealing the *whole track* of spiritual existence. Here, then, is the very genesis of Scientology. *22 lectures.*

THE ROUTE TO INFINITY: TECHNIQUE 80 LECTURES • As Ron explained, "Technique 80 is the *To Be or Not To Be* Technique." With that, he unveiled the crucial foundation on which ability and sanity rest: *the being's capacity to make a decision.* Here, then, is the anatomy of "maybe," the *Wavelengths of ARC*, the *Tone Scale of Decisions*, and the means to rehabilitate a being's ability *To Be ... almost anything.* *7 lectures. (Knowledge of Technique 80 is required for Technique 88 as described in Scientology: A History of Man—below.)*

SCIENTOLOGY: A HISTORY OF MAN • *(This current volume.)* "A cold-blooded and factual account of your last 76 trillion years." So begins A History of Man, announcing the revolutionary *Technique 88*—revealing for the first time the truth about whole track experience and the exclusive address, in auditing, to the thetan. Here is history unraveled with the first E-Meter, delineating and describing the principal incidents on the whole track to be found in any human being: *Electronic implants, entities,* the *genetic track, between-lives incidents, how bodies evolved* and *why you got trapped in them*—they're all detailed here.

TECHNIQUE 88: INCIDENTS ON THE TRACK BEFORE EARTH • "Technique 88 is the most hyperbolical, effervescent, dramatic, unexaggeratable, high-flown, superlative, grandiose, colossal and magnificent technique which the mind of Man could conceivably embrace. It is as big as the whole track and all the incidents on it. It's what you apply it to; it's what's been going on. It contains the riddles and secrets, the mysteries of all time. You could bannerline this technique like they do a sideshow, but nothing you could say, no adjective you could use, would adequately describe even a small segment of it. It not only batters the imagination, it makes you ashamed to imagine anything," is Ron's introduction to you in this never-before-available lecture series, expanding on all else contained in History of Man. What awaits you is the whole track itself. *15 lectures.*

SCIENTOLOGY 8-80 • The *first* explanation of the electronics of human thought and the energy phenomena in any being. Discover how even physical universe laws of motion are mirrored in a being, not to mention the electronics of aberration. Here is the link between theta and MEST revealing what energy *is*, and how you *create* it. It was this breakthrough that revealed the subject of a thetan's *flows* and which, in turn, is applied in *every* auditing process today. In the book's title, "8-8" stands for *Infinity-Infinity,* and "0" represents the static, *theta.* Included are the *Wavelengths of Emotion, Aesthetics, Beauty and Ugliness, Inflow and Outflow* and the *Sub-zero Tone Scale*—applicable only to the thetan.

SOURCE OF LIFE ENERGY • Beginning with the announcement of his new book—Scientology 8-80—Ron not only unveiled his breakthroughs of theta as the Source of Life Energy, but detailed the *Methods of Research* he used to make that and every other discovery of Dianetics and Scientology: the *Qs* and *Logics*—methods of *thinking* applicable to any universe or thinking process. Here, then, is both *how to think* and *how to evaluate all data and knowledge,* and thus, the linchpin to a full understanding of both Scientology and life itself. *14 lectures.*

THE COMMAND OF THETA • While in preparation of his newest book and the Doctorate Course he was about to deliver, Ron called together auditors for a new Professional Course. As he said, "For the first time with this class we are stepping, really, beyond the scope of the word *Survival*." From that vantage point, the Command of Theta gives the technology that bridges the knowledge from 8-80 to 8-8008, and provides the first full explanation of the subject of *Cause* and a permanent shift of orientation in life from MEST to *Theta*. *10 lectures.*

SCIENTOLOGY 8-8008 • The complete description of the behavior and potentials of a *thetan*, and textbook for the Philadelphia Doctorate Course and The Factors: Admiration and the Renaissance of Beingness lectures. As Ron said, the book's title serves to fix in the mind of the individual a route by which he can rehabilitate himself, his abilities, his ethics and his goals—the attainment of *infinity* (8) by the reduction of the apparent *infinity* (8) of the MEST universe to *zero* (0) and the increase of the apparent *zero* (0) of one's own universe to *infinity* (8). Condensed herein are more than 80,000 hours of investigation, with a summarization and amplification of every breakthrough to date—and the full significance of those discoveries form the new vantage point of *Operating Thetan.*

THE PHILADELPHIA DOCTORATE COURSE LECTURES • This renowned series stands as the largest single body of work on the anatomy, behavior and potentials of the spirit of Man ever assembled, providing the very fundamentals which underlie the route to Operating Thetan. Here it is in complete detail—the thetan's relationship to the *creation, maintenance* and *destruction of universes*. In just those terms, here is the *anatomy* of matter, energy, space and time, and *postulating* universes into existence. Here, too, is the thetan's fall from whole track abilities and the *universal laws* by which they are restored. In short, here is Ron's codification of the upper echelon of theta beingness and behavior. Lecture after lecture fully expands every concept of the course text, Scientology 8-8008, providing the total scope of *you* in native state. *76 lectures and accompanying reproductions of the original 54 LRH hand-drawn lecture charts.*

THE FACTORS: ADMIRATION AND THE RENAISSANCE OF BEINGNESS • With the *potentials* of a thetan fully established came a look outward resulting in Ron's monumental discovery of a *universal solvent* and the basic laws of the theta *universe*—laws quite literally senior to anything: *The Factors: Summation of the Considerations of the Human Spirit and Material Universe*. So dramatic were these breakthroughs, Ron expanded the book Scientology 8-8008, both clarifying previous discoveries and adding chapter after chapter which, studied with these lectures, provide a postgraduate level to the Doctorate Course. Here then are lectures containing the knowledge of *universal truth* unlocking the riddle of creation itself. *18 lectures.*

157

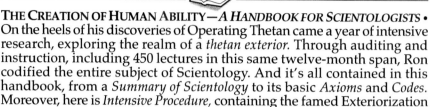

THE CREATION OF HUMAN ABILITY—*A HANDBOOK FOR SCIENTOLOGISTS* •
On the heels of his discoveries of Operating Thetan came a year of intensive
research, exploring the realm of a *thetan exterior.* Through auditing and
instruction, including 450 lectures in this same twelve-month span, Ron
codified the entire subject of Scientology. And it's all contained in this
handbook, from a *Summary of Scientology* to its basic *Axioms* and *Codes.*
Moreover, here is *Intensive Procedure,* containing the famed Exteriorization
Processes of *Route 1* and *Route 2*—processes drawn right from the Axioms.
Each one is described in detail—*how* the process is used, *why* it works, the
axiomatic technology that underlies its use, and the complete explanation
of how a being can break the *false agreements* and *self-created barriers* that
enslave him to the physical universe. In short, this book contains the ultimate
summary of thetan exterior OT ability and its permanent accomplishment.

PHOENIX LECTURES: FREEING THE HUMAN SPIRIT • Here is the
panoramic view of Scientology complete. Having codified the
subject of Scientology in Creation of Human Ability, Ron then delivered
a series of half-hour lectures to specifically accompany a full study
of the book. From the *essentials* that underlie the technology—*The
Axioms, Conditions of Existence and Considerations and Mechanics,* to the
processes of *Intensive Procedure,* including twelve lectures describing
one-by-one the thetan exterior processes of *Route 1*—it's all covered in
full, providing a conceptual understanding of the *science of knowledge*
and *native state OT ability.* Here then are the bedrock principles upon
which everything in Scientology rests, including the embracive
statement of the religion and its heritage—*Scientology, Its General
Background.* Hence, this is the watershed lecture series on Scientology
itself, and the axiomatic foundation for all future research. *42 lectures.*

DIANETICS 55!—*THE COMPLETE MANUAL OF HUMAN COMMUNICATION* •
With all breakthroughs to date, a single factor had been isolated as crucial
to success in every type of auditing. As LRH said, "Communication is so
thoroughly important today in Dianetics and Scientology (as it always has
been on the whole track) that it could be said if you were to get a preclear
into communication, you would get him well." And this book delineates
the *exact,* but previously unknown, anatomy and formulas for *perfect*
communication. The magic of the communication cycle is *the* fundamental
of auditing and the primary reason auditing works. The breakthroughs
here opened new vistas of application—discoveries of such magnitude,
LRH called Dianetics 55! the *Second Book* of Dianetics.

THE UNIFICATION CONGRESS: COMMUNICATION! FREEDOM &
ABILITY • The historic Congress announcing the reunification of the
subjects of Dianetics and Scientology with the release of *Dianetics 55!*
Until now, each had operated in their own sphere: Dianetics addressed
Man *as Man*—the first four dynamics, while Scientology addressed
life itself—the Fifth to Eighth Dynamics. The formula which would
serve as the foundation for all future development was contained in
a single word: *Communication.* It was a paramount breakthrough Ron
would later call, "the great discovery of Dianetics and Scientology."
Here, then, are the lectures, as it happened. *16 lectures and accompanying
reproductions of the original LRH hand-drawn lecture charts.*

SCIENTOLOGY: THE FUNDAMENTALS OF THOUGHT—*THE BASIC BOOK OF THE THEORY AND PRACTICE OF SCIENTOLOGY FOR BEGINNERS* • Designated by Ron as the *Book One of Scientology*. After having fully unified and codified the subjects of Dianetics and Scientology came the refinement of their *fundamentals*. Originally published as a résumé of Scientology for use in translations into non-English tongues, this book is of inestimable value to both the beginner and advanced student of the mind, spirit and life. Equipped with this book alone, one can begin a practice and perform seeming miracle changes in the states of well-being, ability and intelligence of people. Contained within are the *Conditions of Existence, Eight Dynamics, ARC Triangle, Parts of Man*, the full analysis of *Life as a Game*, and more, including exact processes for individual application of these principles in processing. Here, then, in one book, is the starting point for bringing Scientology to people everywhere.

HUBBARD PROFESSIONAL COURSE LECTURES • While Fundamentals of Thought stands as an introduction to the subject for beginners, it also contains a distillation of fundamentals for every Scientologist. Here are the in-depth descriptions of those fundamentals, each lecture one-half hour in length and providing, one-by-one, a complete mastery of a single Scientology breakthrough—*Axioms 1–10; The Anatomy of Control; Handling of Problems; Start, Change and Stop; Confusion and Stable Data; Exteriorization; Valences* and more—the *why* behind them, *how* they came to be and their mechanics. And it's all brought together with the *Code of a Scientologist*, point by point, and its use in actually creating a new civilization. In short, here are the LRH lectures that make a *Professional Scientologist*—one who can apply the subject to every aspect of life. *21 lectures.*

ADDITIONAL BOOKS CONTAINING SCIENTOLOGY ESSENTIALS

WORK

THE PROBLEMS OF WORK—*SCIENTOLOGY APPLIED TO THE WORKADAY WORLD* • Having codified the entire subject of Scientology, Ron immediately set out to provide the *beginning* manual for its application by anyone. As he described it: life is composed of seven-tenths work, one-tenth familial, one-tenth political and one-tenth relaxation. Here, then, is Scientology applied to that seven-tenths of existence including the answers to *Exhaustion* and the *Secret of Efficiency*. Here, too, is the analysis of life itself—a game composed of exact rules. Know them and you succeed. Problems of Work contains technology no one can live without, and that can immediately be applied by both the Scientologist and those new to the subject.

LIFE PRINCIPLES

SCIENTOLOGY: A NEW SLANT ON LIFE • Scientology essentials for every aspect of life. Basic answers that put you in charge of your existence, truths to consult again and again: *Is It Possible to Be Happy?*, *Two Rules for Happy Living, Personal Integrity, The Anti-Social Personality* and many more. In every part of this book you will find Scientology truths that describe conditions in your life and furnish *exact* ways to improve them. Scientology: A New Slant on Life contains essential knowledge for every Scientologist and a perfect introduction for anyone new to the subject.

AXIOMS, CODES AND SCALES

SCIENTOLOGY 0-8: THE BOOK OF BASICS • The companion to *all* Ron's books, lectures and materials. This is *the* Book of Basics, containing indispensable data you will refer to constantly: the *Axioms of Dianetics and Scientology; The Factors;* a full compilation of all *Scales*—more than 100 in all; listings of the *Perceptics* and *Awareness Levels;* all *Codes* and *Creeds* and much more. The senior laws of existence are condensed into this single volume, distilled from more than 15,000 pages of writings, 3,000 lectures and scores of books.

SCIENTOLOGY ETHICS: TECHNOLOGY OF OPTIMUM SURVIVAL

INTRODUCTION TO SCIENTOLOGY ETHICS • A new hope for Man arises with the first workable technology of ethics—technology to help an individual pull himself out of the downward skid of life and to a higher plateau of survival. This is the comprehensive handbook providing the crucial fundamentals: *Basics of Ethics & Justice; Honesty; Conditions of Existence; Condition Formulas* from Confusion to Power; the *Basics of Suppression* and its handling; as well as *Justice Procedures* and their use in Scientology Churches. Here, then, is the technology to overcome any barriers in life and in one's personal journey up the Bridge to Total Freedom.

PURIFICATION

CLEAR BODY, CLEAR MIND—*THE EFFECTIVE PURIFICATION PROGRAM* • We live in a biochemical world, and this book is the solution. While investigating the harmful effects that earlier drug use had on preclears' cases, Ron made the major discovery that many street drugs, particularly LSD, remained in a person's body long after ingested. Residues of the drug, he noted, could have serious and lasting effects, including triggering further "trips." Additional research revealed that a wide range of substances—medical drugs, alcohol, pollutants, household chemicals and even food preservatives—could also lodge in the body's tissues. Through research on thousands of cases, he developed the *Purification Program* to eliminate their destructive effects. Clear Body, Clear Mind details every aspect of the all-natural regimen that can free one from the harmful effects of drugs and other toxins, opening the way for spiritual progress.

REFERENCE HANDBOOKS

WHAT IS SCIENTOLOGY?

The complete and essential encyclopedic reference on the subject and practice of Scientology. Organized for use, this book contains the pertinent data on every aspect of the subject:

• The life of L. Ron Hubbard and his path of discovery

• The Spiritual Heritage of the religion

• A full description of Dianetics and Scientology

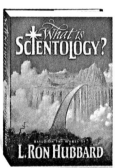

• Auditing—what it is and how it works

• Courses—what they contain and how they are structured

• The Grade Chart of Services and how one ascends to higher states

• The Scientology Ethics and Justice System

• The Organizational Structure of the Church

• A complete description of the many Social Betterment programs supported by the Church, including: Drug Rehabilitation, Criminal Reform, Literacy and Education and the instilling of real values for morality

Over 1,000 pages in length, with more than 500 photographs and illustrations, this text further includes Creeds, Codes, a full listing of all books and materials as well as a Catechism with answers to virtually any question regarding the subject.

You Ask and This Book Answers.

THE SCIENTOLOGY HANDBOOK

Scientology fundamentals for daily use in every part of life. Encompassing 19 separate bodies of technology, here is the most comprehensive manual on the basics of life ever published. Each chapter contains key principles and technology for your continual use:

• Study Technology

• The Dynamics of Existence

• The Components of Understanding— Affinity, Reality and Communication

• The Tone Scale

• Communication and its Formulas

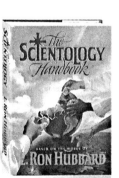

• Assists for Illnesses and Injuries

• How to Resolve Conflicts

• Integrity and Honesty

• Ethics and Condition Formulas

• Answers to Suppression and a Dangerous Environment

• Marriage

• Children

• Tools for the Workplace

More than 700 photographs and illustrations make it easy for you to learn the procedures and apply them at once. This book is truly the indispensable handbook for every Scientologist.

The Technology to Build a Better World.

About L. Ron Hubbard

To really know life," L. Ron Hubbard wrote, "you've got to be part of life. You must get down and look, you must get into the nooks and crannies of existence. You have to rub elbows with all kinds and types of men before you can finally establish what he is."

Through his long and extraordinary journey to the founding of Dianetics and Scientology, Ron did just that. From his adventurous youth in a rough and tumble American West to his far-flung trek across a still mysterious Asia; from his two-decade search for the very essence of life to the triumph of Dianetics and Scientology—such are the stories recounted in the L. Ron Hubbard Biographical Publications.

Presenting the photographic overview of Ron's greater journey is *L. Ron Hubbard: Images of a Lifetime*. Drawn from his own archival collection, this is Ron's life as he himself saw it.

While for the many aspects of that rich and varied life, stands the Ron Series. Each issue focuses on a specific LRH profession: *Auditor, Humanitarian, Philosopher, Artist, Poet, Music Maker, Photographer* and many more including his published articles on *Freedom* and his personal *Letters & Journals*. Here is the life of a man who lived at least twenty lives in the space of one.

For Further Information Visit
www.lronhubbard.org

GUIDE TO THE MATERIALS

YOU'RE ON AN ADVENTURE!
HERE'S THE MAP.

- All books
- All lectures
- All reference books

All of it laid out in chronological sequence with descriptions of what each contains.

*Y*our journey to a full understanding of Dianetics and Scientology is the greatest adventure of all. But you need a map that shows you where you are and where you are going.

That map is the Materials Guide Chart. It shows all Ron's books and lectures with a full description of their content and subject matter so you can find exactly what *you* are looking for and precisely what *you* need.

Since each book and lecture is laid out in chronological sequence, you can see *how* the subjects of Dianetics and Scientology were developed. And what that means is by simply studying this chart you are in for cognition after cognition!

New editions of all books include extensive glossaries, containing definitions for every technical term. And as a result of a monumental restoration program, the entire library of Ron's lectures are being made available on compact disc, with complete transcripts, glossaries, lecture graphs, diagrams and issues he refers to in the lectures. As a result, you get *all* the data, and can learn with ease, gaining a full *conceptual* understanding.

And what that adds up to is a new Golden Age of Knowledge every Dianeticist and Scientologist has dreamed of.

To obtain your FREE Materials Guide Chart and Catalog, or to order L. Ron Hubbard's books and lectures, contact:

WESTERN HEMISPHERE:
Bridge Publications, Inc.
4751 Fountain Avenue
Los Angeles, CA 90029 USA
www.bridgepub.com
Phone: 1-800-722-1733
Fax: 1-323-953-3328

EASTERN HEMISPHERE:
New Era Publications International ApS
Store Kongensgade 53
1264 Copenhagen K, Denmark
www.newerapublications.com
Phone: (45) 33 73 66 66
Fax: (45) 33 73 66 33

Books and lectures are also available direct from Churches of Scientology.
*See **Addresses**.*

ADDRESSES

Scientology is the fastest-growing religion in the world today. Churches and Missions exist in cities throughout the world, and new ones are continually forming.

To obtain more information or to locate the Church nearest you, visit the Scientology website:

www.scientology.org
e-mail: info@scientology.org

or

**Phone: 1-800-334-LIFE
(for US and Canada)**

You can also write to any one of the Continental Organizations, listed on the following page, who can direct you to one of the thousands of Churches and Missions world over.

L. Ron Hubbard's books and lectures may be obtained from any of these addresses or direct from the publishers on the previous page.

CONTINENTAL CHURCH ORGANIZATIONS:

UNITED STATES

CHURCH OF SCIENTOLOGY
CONTINENTAL LIAISON OFFICE
WESTERN UNITED STATES
1308 L. Ron Hubbard Way
Los Angeles, California 90027 USA
info@wus.scientology.org

CHURCH OF SCIENTOLOGY
CONTINENTAL LIAISON OFFICE
EASTERN UNITED STATES
349 W. 48th Street
New York, New York 10036 USA
info@eus.scientology.org

CANADA

CHURCH OF SCIENTOLOGY
CONTINENTAL LIAISON OFFICE
CANADA
696 Yonge Street, 2nd Floor
Toronto, Ontario
Canada M4Y 2A7
info@scientology.ca

LATIN AMERICA

CHURCH OF SCIENTOLOGY
CONTINENTAL LIAISON OFFICE
LATIN AMERICA
Federacion Mexicana de Dianetica
Calle Puebla #31
Colonia Roma, Mexico D.F.
C.P. 06700, Mexico
info@scientology.org.mx

UNITED KINGDOM

CHURCH OF SCIENTOLOGY
CONTINENTAL LIAISON OFFICE
UNITED KINGDOM
Saint Hill Manor
East Grinstead, West Sussex
England, RH19 4JY
info@scientology.org.uk

AFRICA

CHURCH OF SCIENTOLOGY
CONTINENTAL LIAISON OFFICE AFRICA
5 Cynthia Street
Kensington
Johannesburg 2094, South Africa
info@scientology.org.za

167

AUSTRALIA, NEW ZEALAND & OCEANIA

CHURCH OF SCIENTOLOGY
CONTINENTAL LIAISON OFFICE ANZO
16 Dorahy Street
Dundas, New South Wales 2117
Australia
info@scientology.org.au

Church of Scientology
Liaison Office of Taiwan
1st, No. 231, Cisian 2nd Road
Kaoshiung City
Taiwan, ROC
info@scientology.org.tw

EUROPE

CHURCH OF SCIENTOLOGY
CONTINENTAL LIAISON OFFICE EUROPE
Store Kongensgade 55
1264 Copenhagen K, Denmark
info@scientology.org.dk

Church of Scientology
Liaison Office of Commonwealth
of Independent States
Management Center of Dianetics
and Scientology Dissemination
Pervomajskaya Street, House 1A
Korpus Grazhdanskoy Oboroni
Losino-Petrovsky Town
141150 Moscow, Russia
info@scientology.ru

Church of Scientology
Liaison Office of Central Europe
1082 Leonardo da Vinci u. 8-14
Budapest, Hungary
info@scientology.hu

Church of Scientology
Liaison Office of Iberia
C/Miguel Menendez Boneta, 18
28460 – Los Molinos
Madrid, Spain
info@spain.scientology.org

Church of Scientology
Liaison Office of Italy
Via Cadorna, 61
20090 Vimodrone
Milan, Italy
info@scientology.it

BECOME A MEMBER
OF THE INTERNATIONAL
ASSOCIATION OF SCIENTOLOGISTS

The International Association of Scientologists is the membership organization of all Scientologists united in the most vital crusade on Earth.

A free Six-Month Introductory Membership is extended to anyone who has not held a membership with the Association before.

As a member, you are eligible for discounts on Scientology materials offered only to IAS Members. You also receive the Association magazine, *IMPACT*, issued six times a year, full of Scientology news from around the world.

The purpose of the IAS is:

"To unite, advance, support and protect Scientology and Scientologists in all parts of the world so as to achieve the Aims of Scientology as originated by L. Ron Hubbard."

Join the strongest force for positive change on the planet today, opening the lives of millions to the greater truth embodied in Scientology.

JOIN THE INTERNATIONAL
ASSOCIATION OF SCIENTOLOGISTS.
To apply for membership,
write to the International
Association of Scientologists
c/o Saint Hill Manor, East Grinstead
West Sussex, England, RH19 4JY

www.iasmembership.org

EDITOR'S GLOSSARY
OF WORDS, TERMS AND PHRASES

Words often have several meanings. The definitions used here only give the meaning that the word has as it is used in this book. Dianetics and Scientology terms appear in bold type. Beside each definition you will find the page on which it first appears, so you can refer back to the text if you wish.

This glossary is not meant to take the place of standard language or Dianetics and Scientology dictionaries, which should be referred to for any words, terms or phrases that do not appear below.

—The Editors

acceptance–rejection confusions: instances about being confused as to whether to accept or reject something. Page 44.

accounts (for): gives a satisfactory reason (for); explains. Page 41.

Achaea: an ancient district in southern Greece. Early in the fourth century B.C. the twelve cities of Achaea formed a military alliance, including non-Achaean allies, which later became the chief political power in Greece. Page 41.

act up: behave in an unexpected or uncontrolled way; misbehave. Page 132.

after a fashion: in some way but not very well. Page 74.

agile: characterized by quickness, lightness and ease of movement; well-coordinated. Page 51.

algae: any of several divisions of simple organisms having no true root, stem or leaf. Algae are found in water or damp places and include seaweed and pond scum. Page 44.

all in all: everything considered; in general. Page 22.

ambidextrous: able to use both hands equally well. Page 40.

amperage: the strength of a current of electricity expressed in amperes (a standard unit for measuring the rate of flow of an electric current, that is, how much electricity is flowing per unit of time, such as per second). Page 71.

ampere(s): a standard unit for measuring the rate of flow of an electric current, that is, how much electricity is flowing per unit of time, such as per second. The typical light bulb uses ½ an ampere and a toaster about 12 amperes. Page 90.

anaten: *anaten* is short for *analytical attenuation. Attenuation* is the action of weakening or reducing in force or intensity. Page 56.

anesthetized: deprived of sensation; unconscious. Page 40.

-anities: a coined word from *-ity,* which is combined with other words to form nouns that express the quality or state of something. For instance *human* plus *-ity* equals *humanity,* the condition or quality of being human, *Christian* plus *-ity* equals *Christianity,* the state or fact of being a Christian. Hence "-anities" is a reference to the many beingnesses and schools of thought with which Man has approached the problems of Man. Page 64.

antediluvian: of or belonging to the time before the Great Flood—the universal deluge recorded as having occurred in the days of Noah. Front Cover.

anthropoid: a manlike ape, such as the gorilla and chimpanzee. Page 41.

antipathetic: feeling or expressing anger, hostility, strong opposition or disgust, especially toward a particular person or thing. Page 20.

anxiety stomach: a quivery stomach whenever anything goes wrong; *anxiety* means distress or uneasiness of mind caused by fear of danger or misfortune. Page 20.

appertains to: relates to or concerns. Page 104.

approximation: a method of knowing and thinking by making a mock-up. One creates a thought mock-up that approximates a situation that one wants to solve or do something about. It is not even a facsimile, it is so minute, its wavelength is so tiny, that he doesn't even know that it is there. He makes changes to this thought mock-up in order to figure out a solution to the problem. Approximation is described in the lecture series *Technique 88: Incidents on the Track Before Earth.* Page 71.

Archimedes: (ca. 287–212 B.C.) Greek mathematician and inventor. He was asked by a king to determine whether a crown was pure gold or mixed with silver. When he found the answer, he was so excited by his discovery he ran out into the street shouting Eureka! (I have found it!) Page 1.

ARC Processing: processing in which the auditor has the preclear recall moments when he actually felt he was receiving or giving affinity or communication, or actually experiencing reality. This type of processing is covered in *Self Analysis*. Page 33.

Arsclycus: an old society built in space, with no planet, in which there were many roads, turrets, castles, and so forth. People were brought in and put to work there. Every time they died, they found themselves standing back in the same line again and were slipped back into a body for about ten thousand consecutive lifetimes until Arsclycus blew up. Page 116.

arthritis: inflammation of the joints, causing pain, swelling and stiffness. Page 6.

artifact: any object made by human beings, sometimes left over from a previous time period and is of interest. Page 27.

ascendancy: a position of power or domination over others. Page 40.

assist: the straight perception-by-perception running, over and over, of an accident or incident until it is desensitized as a facsimile and cannot affect the preclear. The assist is used immediately after accidents or operations. It takes away shock and most of the harmful effects of the incident and promotes healing. It is done by starting the individual at the beginning of the incident, with the first awareness of the incident, just as though the preclear were living it all the way through again with full perception of sight, sound, etc., as nearly as they can be obtained. An assist run, for instance, immediately after a dental operation takes all the shock out of the operation. One concludes an assist by picking up the auditing as another incident and running through the auditing and the decision to be audited. An assist saves lives and materially speeds healing. Page 18.

as the case may be: according to the circumstances (used when referring to two or more possible alternatives). Page 101.

at (the) (very) least: used to add a positive comment about a situation that could be negative, or to mean, even if nothing else is true or one does nothing else, as in *"Here, at the very least, is the explanation," "volcanoes which, at the least, were spectacular," "being able to at least assist the survival."* Page 41.

at length: after some time; eventually. Page 47.

atom: a tiny basic building block of matter which is the smallest unit of matter that can take part in a chemical reaction. Atoms are made of smaller particles called electrons, protons and neutrons. An atom consists of a cloud of electrons (negatively charged particles) surrounding and moving about a small, dense nucleus (center) of protons and neutrons. Protons are particles that carry a positive charge of electricity and neutrons are particles that have no electrical charge. Page 43.

Attention Unit Running: a technique in which the auditor runs the preclear on fixing and unfixing attention units, without having to hook up with a facsimile. With this done, incidents will show up. It makes it possible to run incidents below the level of perception. Attention Unit Running is described in the lecture series *Technique 88: Incidents on the Track Before Earth*. Page 86.

attention units: energy flows of small wavelengths and definite frequency; quantities of awareness. Page 11.

at will: just as or when one wishes. Page 72.

aura: the theta body and its energy. Page 99.

baboon: a large ground-dwelling type of monkey native to Africa and Asia with a long snout (resembling that of a dog), large teeth, a short tail, bare pink patches on the buttocks, and with arms about as long as its legs. Baboons range in weight from 24 pounds (11 kilograms) to 90 pounds (41 kilograms). Page 51.

Babylonia: an ancient empire in southwest Asia (located in what is now southern Iraq) that flourished from 2100 to 689 B.C. and again (as Chaldea or New Babylonia) from 625 to 538 B.C. Babylonia produced the first form of writing, a set of laws, and studies in mathematics, astronomy and other sciences. Page 41.

back track: the whole span of time comprising a being's existence prior to the current lifetime. Page 3.

backwoods: an area that is far from population centers or that is held to be culturally backward. Page 38.

bad off: in a bad or poor condition or circumstance. Page 128.

bale: literally, a large bundle or package prepared for shipping, storage, etc. Figuratively, a large amount or quantity. Page 62.

bank: the mental image picture collection which forms the storage system of the mind, an analogy to memory storage in a computer. Page 79.

baps: electronic waves fired at an individual during an implant. The word *baps* is used to imitate the stuttering sounds of such an action. Page 104.

barnacle: a small marine organism with a shell that clings to rocks and ships and draws food by extending slender hairs through its shell to catch small organisms. It stays in one position during its adult life. Page 47.

basic: a series of similar engrams, or of similar locks, are called *chains*. A *basic* is the first incident (engram, lock, overt act) on any chain. Page 18.

bear(s) up: confirm(s) as true or valid after being examined or looked into. Page 6.

beauty: beauty is a wavelength closely resembling theta or a harmony approximating theta. The description of beauty and its use in auditing is contained in *Scientology 8-80*. *See also* **ugliness**. Page 143.

begetting: procreating or generating offspring. Page 65.

behooves: is necessary or proper for; is advantageous. Page 32.

belligerently: in a manner showing readiness to fight or quarrel. Page 42.

bereft: deprived, especially by death; stripped. Page 129.

betokening: indicating; giving evidence of. Page 107.

between-lives: at death, the theta being leaves the body and goes to the between-lives area. Here he "reports in," is given a strong forgetter implant and is then shot down to a body just before it is born. The subject is described in the lecture series *Technique 88: Incidents on the Track Before Earth*. Page 27.

bibliophile: a person who loves or collects books. Page 79.

biology: the science of the origin, development, physical characteristics, habits, etc., of living forms. Page 18.

bivalve: a type of mollusk such as oysters and clams. The usage derives from the Latin word *valva* which means one half of a double door. A *valve* in this case is one of the paired, hinged shells of the mollusk. The two shells are drawn together by muscles attached to their inner surfaces. Page 40.

"black band" waves: gross (thick, dense) waves that cannot be seen or heard and which are used to inflict pain. Page 88.

Blanketing: Blanketing is described in Chapter Nine, section on "Blanketing." Page 81.

bloom, in full: in full force or operation; at its peak or point of highest development, strength, etc., likened to a flower that is in full bloom, meaning fully open. Hence, fully active or in (full) restimulation. Page 116.

blow-out area: a region where a blowout occurs or can occur. A *blowout* is a sudden bursting of something caused by the internal pressure of material contained inside it, as when a tire bursts due to the pressure of the contained air on a weak spot. Page 47.

blows, ill will that: evil or hostile feeling or intention (ill will) that happens to come along, bringing misfortune to anyone it strikes. The phrase alludes to the idea of an *ill wind that blows,* a force that brings misfortune or disaster. *Wind* in this sense means a force, influence or tendency that drives or carries something along, or to which one is exposed. Page 62.

blow (something) off the map: to destroy completely or out of existence. Literally, to obliterate by explosion (blow) so that something no longer could be located on a map. Page 73.

board: something that is solid and stiff, likened to a wooden *board,* a long, flat slab of sawed lumber which is hard and inflexible. Page 104.

body in pawn: a body held in one place, hypnotized or knocked out, where the person is told that he belongs *here,* but he must go over *here* and live. The body is floating in fluid or under a constant electronic bath. They're lying on a pallet or something of the sort; the body is completely motionless. He's just nebulously monitored by that body, because somebody can walk in, stir up the body, give the body a command, and he himself will perceive the command. Described in the lecture series *Technique 88: Incidents on the Track Before Earth.* See also Chapter Nine, section on "The Double-Body." Page 107.

bogged: mired down, sunk in or as if in a bog (wet, spongy ground). Page 4.

boil-off: the manifestation of former periods of unconsciousness, accompanied by grogginess. In its English usage, *boil-off* refers to the reduction of quantity of a liquid by its conversion to a gaseous state, such as steam. Boil-off is described in *Dianetics: The Modern Science of Mental Health.* Page 137.

Boohoo: a name derived from the word *boohoo*, an informal word used to express the sound made by noisy crying (weeping). Page 49.

borrow(ed)(ing): borrowing is described in Chapter Nine, section on "Borrowing." Page 79.

bound-in: limited or confined within some place, position, state, etc. Page 74.

bring (something) to light: make something widely known or evident; reveal or publish something. Page 89.

broil: confused, violent agitation. Page 47.

brutal: 1. unpleasantly precise or penetrating. Page 4.
2. unfeeling and cruel. Page 63.

bulbous: having round, bulging parts. A reference to types of seaweeds which contain small or large air-filled sacs that keep them afloat. Page 45.

bulk, in the: in the majority or greater part of something. Page 75.

bumper: a device like the big bar that projects out from the front and rear of a motor vehicle for absorbing some of the shock of a collision. It is usually metal, plastic or hard rubber. Page 62.

business: 1. that with which a person is concerned such as a task, duty or function undertaken toward a specific end, as in *"It became my business to discover, against considerable odds, that truth."* Page 3.
2. an activity engaged in as a normal or unavoidable part of something and usually extending over a period of time, as in *"They can be any combination of action known to the business of living."* Page 30.

business, go about one's: attend to one's own affairs; do the things one normally does. Page 45.

busy, get: become engaged in or occupied with; become active. Page 1.

but to, no choice: a phrase meaning, one cannot do anything except, as in *"the auditor has no choice but to audit it."* Page 42.

by the way: used to introduce something that is not strictly part of the subject at hand; in passing as a side topic. Page 42.

calisthenics: gymnastic exercises designed to develop physical health and vigor, usually performed with little or no special apparatus. Page 30.

call (to action): an invitation or appeal to undertake a particular course of action. Page 1.

cancer, embryonic: a form of cancer in which reproductive cells in the body, such as sperm, eventually develop into cancer cells. *Embryonic* means relating to or characteristic of an *embryo*, a human offspring in initial developmental stage. *Cancer* is a disease in which abnormal cells multiply wildly in the body and destroy healthy tissue, thereby endangering the body. Page 31.

cancer—malignant cell: a disease in which cells multiply wildly in the body and destroy healthy tissue. *Malignant* in its medical sense means likely to grow or spread harmfully. A *cell* is the smallest independently functioning unit in the body. It is the uncontrolled reproduction of malignant cells invading healthy areas of the body that causes damage. Page 31.

cap: 1. a protective cover or seal that closes off one end of something. Page 47.
2. a closefitting covering that fits over the head. Page 144.

carbon-oxygen engine: a motor which operates on carbon and oxygen. In the body of a human, or any mammal, oxygen from the air and carbon from food are mixed together to form energy which is then used. Page 19.

carnivorous: feeding mainly on the flesh of other animals; meat-eating. Page 51.

carried somebody through: helped somebody (or something) survive a difficult period. Page 4.

cellular: having to do with a *cell*, the smallest structural unit of an organism that is capable of independent functioning. All plants and animals are made up materially of one or more cells that usually combine to form various tissues. For instance the human body has more than 10 trillion cells. Page 18.

Chaldea: an ancient region that formed the southern part of Babylonia. Chaldea eventually took control of Babylonia and brought about a vast civilization called the New Babylonian Empire (625 to 538 B.C.). The region expanded and became the center of the civilized world. The city of Babylon was rebuilt during this period, adding new walls, temples and ornamentation. It became wealthy through commerce and became the largest city of the known world. Page 41.

charge: a store or accumulation of energy. Page 40.

charge: an accumulation of electrical energy. Page 73.

charge notation: from *notation,* the act of noting or making a record (of something). *Charge notation* refers to the fact that a thetan will sometimes park his incidents on the time track and assign those incidents to orderly positions for his notations' sake. Page 79.

charlatanism: the practice or method of one who pretends to have expert knowledge or skill but is in fact a fake. Page 98.

Chart of Attitudes: a chart which notes the ideal state of being and one's attitudes and reactions in life. The Chart of Attitudes is contained in the book *Handbook for Preclears.* Page 90.

check: 1. to make an inquiry, examination, etc., as for verification, as in *"However, it must be remarked that individual cells have 'past lives,' the easiest manifestation of past lives to check."* Page 18.
2. to prove to be right; correspond accurately, as in *"The migrations of a single cell throughout the body are very easy to track in this fashion and ordinarily check against standard suppositions in the field of physical biology."* Page 18.
3. an inquiry, search or examination, as in *"A check on psychotics recently showed five, taken at random, to have been 'triggered' by a threat of arrest a short time before the psychotic break occurred."* Page 105.

choice but to, no: a phrase meaning, one cannot do anything except, as in *"the auditor has no choice but to audit it."* Page 42.

circuit: a pseudopersonality out of a facsimile strong enough to dictate to the individual and BE the individual. For a full explanation of circuits, see *Dianetics: The Modern Science of Mental Health.* Page 22.

Clam: an incident on the genetic line. The Clam is described in Chapter Four, section on "The Clam." Page 42.

clean slate: a new start or fresh chance. A *slate* is a thin piece or plate of rock used for writing on with chalk. From the practice in nineteenth-century taverns of recording a customer's debts on a slate with a chalk. Once the debt was paid, the record would be wiped off and the customer had a "clean slate." A person's experiences have often been compared to the writing accumulated on a slate. Page 110.

coitus: sexual intercourse. Page 30.

cold-blooded: rational; straightforward and not fanciful or emotional. Page 3.

College: the Hubbard College in Phoenix, Arizona, where in 1952 auditors were trained on professional courses. The College had some twelve Associates throughout the country. Each one of them had its own professional courses, played lecture tapes, gave professional processing and distributed books. See *Addresses* for current locations. Page 11.

colonization: the action of colonizing (creating a colony), moving a group of people from their native country, home or planet and settling them in a distant place and often under the control of the original country or planet. Page 106.

color: alter or influence to some degree; to cause to appear different from the reality. Page 22.

command post: *see* **control center(s)**.

comments: remarks on or upon (often unfavorably). Page 6.

complexity: the condition of being difficult to understand, or being made up of many interrelated things. Page 17.

composite: something made of separate parts or elements. Page 19.

computations: the action or result of keeping facsimiles in present time to think with them. Page 133.

Concept Running: processing where the preclear "gets the idea" of *knowing* or *not being* and holds it, the while looking at his time track. The concept runs out or the somatic it brings on runs out and the concept itself is run. It is not addressed at individual incidents but at hundreds. Page 61.

conduit: transmit or convey as through a pipe or channel. Page 47.

cone: any object or space having the shape of a *cone*, an object that has a broad circular base at one end and comes to a point at the other, such as an ice-cream cone. Hence, a *"cone of force"* refers to a force in the shape of a cone. Page 100.

connotations: ideas or meanings suggested by or associated with (something). Page 145.

contagion: the transmission or communication of a disease from body to body. Hence, by extension, the transference and spreading of harmful or corrupting influences from one thing to another. Page 92.

control center(s): 1. "The control center of the organism can be defined as the contact point between *theta* and the physical universe and is that center which is aware of being aware and which has charge of and responsibility for the organism along all its dynamics." Axiom 125, from *Handbook for Preclears*.

2. "the Control Center of the left side of the mind-brain system runs the right side of the body. And the right side of the mind-brain system runs the left side of the body. Thus the mind solved the difficulties of the double control center condition which began about the time Man's forebears began to emerge from the sea, or shortly before. One of these control centers is the 'genetic' boss. It is stronger than the other control center. A natural right-hander is running on his left control center and it is natively the most powerful control center of the body. In such a case, the opposite control center is obedient to the chief control center and all is well, coordination is good and no confusions result. Take a natural left-hander, however, who is running on his right control center and insist that he change to his right hand and you force him to become controlled by his sub-control center. You invalidate his more powerful control center. This causes him to go down the Tone Scale and it causes poor physical coordination between left and right hands." From *Handbook for Preclears*. The subject and description of control centers are contained in *Handbook for Preclears* and its companion lecture series *The Life Continuum*. Page 40.

conversant: familiar with as from experience or study. Page 85.

cool: diminish or reduce the intensity of something, such as a feeling, an awareness, etc. Page 61.

copyrights of Dianetics, efforts on the part of some to acquire and own the: referring to a group in the early 1950s, headed by a wealthy businessman who attempted to seize control of the name and copyrights of Dianetics so he might capitalize on the subject for personal profit. Page 6.

Coronet: a pocket-sized general interest American magazine published from 1936 to 1961. Page 28.

cosmic: of or pertaining to outer space or the physical universe other than Earth. Page 43.

cosmic rays: electrically charged, high-energy particles such as those emitted from an exploding sun or star. Page 43.

costs, at all: whatever effort is needed; in spite of all losses; whatever happens. Page 46.

counter-: a word used in combination with another with the meaning of against, in opposition or response to; opposite. Page 11.

counter-effort: the efforts of the environment (physical) against the individual. The individual's own effort is simply called *effort*. The efforts of the environment are called *counter-efforts*. The subject of counter-effort can be found in *Handbook for Preclears* and its companion lecture series *The Life Continuum*. Page 11.

counter-emotion: the emotion around you. The "atmosphere" around you, the emotion of others toward you. The subject of counter-emotion can be found in *Handbook for Preclears* and its companion lecture series *The Life Continuum*. Page 11.

counter-mis-emotionalism: the action or conduct of someone being mis-emotional against one. Emotion is simply transferred by anger, fear, argument, sympathy, etc., from a mis-emotion person into the facsimiles of another. You can become less sure of yourself or uneasy around people who are embarrassed or uneasy or afraid. You are getting your facsimiles "colored" by a foreign emotion. Every facsimile you advance, with argument or persuasion, toward a mis-emotional person gets counter-emotion thrown into it. Mis-emotionalism and counter-mis-emotionalism are the overt and motivator invalidations on the emotion level. *Counter* means against, contrary or opposite. *See also* **mis-emotionalism**. Page 91.

counters: acts in response to and by, or as if by, striking with a force that attempts to overcome an action or move on the part of an attacking opponent. Page 100.

counter-thought: you think one thing, somebody else thinks another. Their thought is counter to your thought. The subject of counter-thought can be found in *Handbook for Preclears* and its companion lecture series *The Life Continuum*. Page 11.

counter-units: a flow of attention units which counteract another flow of attention units from the same being. For example, an individual consciously starts to create a flow of attention units, they hit these facsimiles which he is carefully holding in place from some other source or quarter, and the attention units which he is trying to put out, almost before they can be formed, are being stopped by the wall of attention units which are mocking up the old facsimile. Page 85.

coupled: combined or connected with (something else). Page 11.

covert: concealed, hidden or disguised; not openly practiced or shown. Page 121.

cover-up: having to do with an effort or a carefully devised plan of concealing something or preventing something from being known. Page 81.

cowed: frightened into submission or obedience. Page 132.

craniums: skulls. Page 89.

creature: 1. person; human being. Page 4.
2. an animal, as distinct from a human being. Page 46.

credible: capable of being believed or accepted (as true). Page 1.

crustacean: chiefly a water animal, having no backbone, many jointed legs and a hard external shell, such as a crab or lobster.

cult: great or excessive devotion or dedication to some person, idea or thing. Page 64.

cult, new: a reference to early Christianity which emerged in the midst of older established religions with the belief that God had created the world and created Man from the dust of Earth and all animals from the ground. During the first five hundred years after Christ and before the birth of the prophet Mohammed (founder of Islam), missionaries spread Christianity eastward across the old Persian Empire (30° to 80° East Longitude, 30° North Latitude). Page 38.

cunning: inventive skill or imagination in doing something; cleverness. Page 28.

curiosa: things which arouse interest but may not be of vital importance. Page 28.

cytology: the study of cells, their formation, structure and function. Page 38.

dampen: reduce or lessen the energy or action of something. Page 99.

Darwin: Charles Darwin (1809–1882), English naturalist and author. His book *On the Origin of Species* proposed a theory to explain evolution of life forms to higher forms. Page 37.

DED: *DED* stands for *DEserveD* action, an incident the preclear does to another dynamic and for which he has no motivator—i.e., he punishes or hurts or wrecks something the like of which has never hurt him. Now he must justify the incident. He will use things which didn't happen to him. He claims that the object of his injury really deserved it, hence the word, which is a sarcasm. See Chapter Ten. Page 17.

deduced: formed as a conclusion from things already observed or known. Page 47.

degradation: the state of being brought down, lowered or reduced, physically or mentally. Page 32.

degree, some: to a certain extent or amount; somewhat. Page 11.

demon circuits: in Dianetics, a "demon" is a parasitic circuit. It has an action in the mind which approximates another entity than self and was considered in Dianetics to be derived entirely from words in engrams. Their phenomena are described in *Dianetics: The Modern Science of Mental Health*. Page 20.

depravity: state of being morally bad, corrupt or wicked. Page 66.

dials, drop as much as twenty (or five): a *drop* is the movement of the needle on the E-Meter to the right as one faces it. A drop of five or twenty dials would mean that the needle kept falling a full dial each of the five or twenty times the Tone Arm was moved to bring the needle back on the dial, indicating something is very heavily charged. Page 40.

dimension: a measurement in space such as length, width or height. Hence "another dimension" is outside the physical universe that can be measured. Page 73.

diplomas: certificates issued by an educational institution (school, university, etc.) certifying that the person has satisfactorily completed a course of study. Page 7.

dismembered: had one's limbs (arms or legs) torn, cut or pulled off. Page 73.

dispersal of energy: attention units of the thetan going out in all directions. Page 50.

disposed to: willing or likely to do something. Page 98.

divergence: difference (between two or more things). Also, separating and going in different directions. Page 27.

dividend: the return or reward resulting from an activity, effort or undertaking. Page 12.

do-gooders: people who seek to correct social ills in an idealistic but usually impractical or superficial way. Page 116.

doomsday: in traditional Christianity, the day at the end of the world when God judges all human beings, sending the saved to Heaven and the damned to Hell. Hence, the last day of the world's existence. Page 131.

double-hinge: a reference to the two hinges of a clam. A *hinge* is a movable joint or mechanism by which something opens or closes or which connects linked objects. In a clam, one hinge serves to open the shell and the other hinge in the same vicinity serves to align the shell when it is closing and to lock it in place. Page 46.

douche: a stream of water, often containing medicinal or cleansing agents, that is applied to a body part or cavity for hygienic or therapeutic purposes. Also the instrument, as a syringe, for administering it. Page 30.

down to a very fine point: mastered completely and perfectly. *Point* in this sense is a specified degree, condition. Page 89.

downview: a sight of something as from a higher to a lower position; a downward look. Page 56.

drafts: currents of uncomfortably cold air penetrating a room or other space. Page 32.

dramatis personae: the participants in an actual event or series of events or the persons in an engram. *Dramatis personae* is Latin and literally means people (or persons) of a drama. Page 27.

drives in: forces something into a place or position. Page 87.

drop as much as twenty (or five) dials: a *drop* is the movement of the needle on the E-Meter to the right as one faces it. A drop of five or twenty dials would mean that the needle kept falling a full dial each of the five or twenty times the Tone Arm was moved to bring the needle back on the dial, indicating something is very heavily charged. Page 40.

drop out: withdraw or disappear from its position or place in something; disappear from notice. Page 108.

drowns: overwhelms or causes to disappear as if by submerging in water. Page 112.

dually: in a double capacity, in two ways. Page 29.

dub-in: a term used to characterize vision or recall which is imaginary. The term comes from the motion-picture industry. To "dub," in moviemaking, is to create and add sounds to a picture after filming is complete. This process ("dubbing") results in a fabricated soundtrack that *seems* to the audience like it actually took place when filmed.

185

But in fact, much, or *all* of it, was created in the studio long after filming was finished, and was then "dubbed in." Hence, *dub-in* is something put there that seems like it happened, but in reality it did not. Page 50.

due: in accord with what is right; proper or appropriate. Page 43.

dumpy: having a short and plump build or shape. Page 105.

dwindling spiral: a three-dimensional "vicious circle" which carries the individual down the Tone Scale. It is so called because the more entheta there is on the case, the more theta will be turned into entheta at each new restimulation. *Spiral* here refers to a progressive downward movement, marking a relentlessly deteriorating state of affairs, and considered to take the form of a spiral. The term comes from aviation where it is used to describe the phenomenon of a plane descending and spiraling in smaller and smaller circles, as in an accident or feat of expert flying, which if not handled can result in loss of control and a crash. Page 66.

eccentrically: in an irregular and erratic manner. Page 114.

effort: the physical-force manifestation of motion. A sharp effort against an individual produces pain. A strenuous effort produces discomfort. Effort can be recalled and re-experienced by the preclear. The essential part of a painful facsimile is its effort, not its perceptions. See *Advanced Procedure and Axioms.* Page 11.

8.0: reference to exhilaration, at 8.0 on the Emotional Tone Scale. Page 72.

80: short for *Technique 80*, the cultivation of disintegration of engrams instead of going over them and over them and over them. Technique 80 doesn't have very much to do with facsimiles or their erasure or running on a time track. One simply disintegrates the engrams. It is a development of that facility. The Technique 80 lectures containing the complete description of this technology are available as *The Route to Infinity.* Page 86.

Einstein: Albert Einstein (1879–1955), German-born American physicist whose theories on the nature of mass and energy led to development of the atomic bomb. Page 6.

electroencephalograph: an instrument for measuring and recording the electric activity of the brain; from Greek *electro*, electric, *encephalo*, in the head, plus *graph*, an instrument for recording information. Page 6.

electroniced down: to be given an electronic implant. The phrase, *electroniced down,* is a coined expression from the phrase *mow down,* which literally means to destroy or kill indiscriminately, as in "the troops were *mowed down* by the enemy." Hence, as thetans were injured with electronics, they were "electroniced down." Page 113.

electronic incidents: incidents containing use of electronics. Electronic incidents are described in Chapters Eight and Nine. Page 20.

electronic microscope: a microscope of extremely high power that uses beams of electrons instead of rays of light, the magnified image being formed on a video screen or recorded in a photograph. Its magnification is much greater than that of a regular microscope. Page 6.

electronic mutation: *mutation* is a random change in the hereditary material of an organism's cells resulting in a new trait or characteristic, as distinguished from a variation resulting from generations of gradual change. Various influences can cause the hereditary material to change, one of which can be electronic particles whether from direct contact of the body or through beams or rays. This change is then passed on to the organism's offspring. Page 38.

electronics: pertaining to *electronics,* the science dealing with the development and application of devices and systems involving the flow of electrical energy in vacuums, gases and solids. Page 6.

electronics: reference to electronic incidents—incidents of tremendous force, marked by the use of heavy electrical currents. Electronic incidents are described in Chapters Eight and Nine. Page 73.

electronics engineer: one trained in the application of the principles of electronics for practical purposes. *Electronics* is the science dealing with the development and application of devices and systems involving the flow of electrical energy in vacuums, gases and solids. Page 6.

Electropsychometer: the full name for an E-Meter. (*Electro* means electric or electricity, *psycho* means soul, and *meter* means measure.) Page 6.

Electropsychometric Auditing: the first operator's manual for the E-Meter, published in 1952. (*Electro* means electric or electricity, *psycho* means soul, and *meter* means measure.) Available in the *Technical Bulletins* volumes and the *Technique 88: Incidents on the Track Before Earth* lecture series package supplement. Page 11.

elsewise: in some other manner; otherwise. Page 113.

embraced: included or contained as part of something broader. Page 12.

embryonic cancer: a form of cancer in which reproductive cells in the body, such as sperm, eventually develop into cancer cells. *Embryonic* means relating to or characteristic of an *embryo*, a human offspring in initial developmental stage. *Cancer* is a disease in which abnormal cells multiply wildly in the body and destroy healthy tissue, thereby endangering the body. Page 31.

E-Meter: short for *electropsychometer,* a specially designed instrument used by an auditor which helps locate long-hidden sources of travail. It does not diagnose or cure anything; it simply measures the mental state or change of state of an individual. Page 1.

emoting: showing or portraying emotion. Page 128.

emotion: the catalyst used by the theta being to monitor physical action. It is used by thought to effect effort. There are many emotions. The principal ones are happiness, boredom, antagonism, anger, covert hostility, fear, grief and apathy. The subject of emotion can be found in *Advanced Procedure and Axioms* and its companion lecture series *Thought, Emotion and Effort.* Page 11.

emotional curve: that drop or rise on the Tone Scale attend to failure to control on any dynamic or to the recipient of an ally on any dynamic. The drop falls from above 2.5 down to apathy in a steep curve. It occurs in seconds or minutes or hours. The speed of its fall is an index of the severity of the failure. (*Attend* means associated with something or resulting or following from it.) Emotional curve is fully described in *Advanced Procedure and Axioms.* Page 101.

empire(s): the country, region, or union of states or territories under the control of an emperor or other powerful leader or government. An *empire* is a group of conquered or colonized states, each with its own government under the empire as a whole. (A *colony* is a country or area separate from but ruled by another country.) Page 41.

end: the ultimate goal; the most important thing, as in *"they are no end of existence."* Page 22.

energy: in physics, the ability something has to work or move. Page 11.

energy, the three actions of: there are only three actions of energy: it can flow; it can form ridges and it can disperse. The three actions of energy are fully described in the lecture series *Technique 88: Incidents on the Track Before Earth.* Page 11.

engram: a recording of a moment of pain and unconsciousness. The complete description of engrams is contained in *Dianetics: The Modern Science of Mental Health*. Page 18.

engulf: to swallow up, cover over, surround or overwhelm, as if by overflowing and enclosing. Page 63.

entity: something that exists separately from other things and has its own identity. Page 19.

eons: ages, an indefinitely long period of time. Page 37.

epicenters: focal points, as of activity. From *epi* (on, over, near) and *center*. *Epicenter* is taken from its derivation, meaning center on the center, and is a study of successive command posts of a human organism. "At the origin of each new organism it is postulated that its new control center is in complete control of the organism and environment and will be obeyed by all the sub-control centers of the organism. In a new organism, it is postulated that its new control center is going to be in command of the organism in this generation. It is going to be obeyed by all old sub-centers." From the *Logics and Axioms* lecture of 11 October 1951, "Epicenters and Self-determinism," in the *Thought, Emotion and Effort* lecture series. Page 39.

Eureka: Greek for "I have found it." Page 1.

evaporate: disappear or vanish; fade away to nothing. Page 53.

even: to make level, flat or smooth, as a road, so as to be easier to travel. Used figuratively. Page 27.

evidence, in: actually present; plainly visible; easily seen or noticed. Page 43.

evolutionary: of or pertaining to *evolution*, the idea that all living things evolved from simple organisms and changed through the ages to produce millions of different species: the theory that development of a species or organism from its original or primitive state to its present state includes adaptation (form or structure modified to better survive and multiply in a changed environment). Page 12.

evolution, theory of: the idea that all living things evolved from simple organisms and changed through the ages to produce millions of different species: the theory that development of a species or organism from its original or primitive state to its present state includes adaptation (form or structure modified to better survive and multiply in a changed environment). Page 37.

189

evolved: worked out or developed especially by experience, experimentation or intensive care or effort. Page 5.

extraterrestrial: coming from outside Earth. Page 42.

eyes, in (one's) own: in one's own opinion, estimation or judgment; from one's own point of view. Page 91.

Facsimile One: an electronic incident on the whole track. This incident is fully described in Chapter Nine, section on "Facsimile One." Page 32.

factors: the elements contributing to a particular result or situation. Page 17.

faddist: one who indulges in fads (something that is taken up with exaggerated enthusiasm, especially by many people and which is usually short-lived), as unusual diets, beliefs, etc. Page 50.

fall: that part of the year when leaves fall from the trees (hence, *fall*) and that comes after summer and before winter; autumn. Page 1.

far as, so: 1. used to give facts or an opinion about a particular aspect of something noted. Page 5.
2. to the degree or extent that. Page 18.

fashion, in this (or such): in the way or manner indicated. Page 18.

favor of, in: on the side of; in support of. Page 3.

fervor: originally the word meant intense heat. Hence, powerful, intense emotion, feeling, expression or enthusiasm toward or about something, as in *"religious fervor."* Page 103.

fester: to cause something to become infected, making it worse. Used figuratively to describe a worsening of something already bad. Page 63.

festering: becoming an increasing source of irritation or poisoning; becoming infected, inflamed or corrupted. Page 63.

field: a region, volume or space where a specific, measurable influence, force, etc., exists. Page 22.

fifth dimension: a theoretical dimension beyond or in addition to a fourth dimension. *See also* **fourth dimension.** Page 73.

fifth nerve channel: a nerve on each side of the head which emerges from the base of the brain and travels to the face, sinuses, eyes and teeth. It is the fifth and largest of twelve nerves that travel out of the brain. Page 47.

file-card system: literally, a highly structured arrangement of information, in which a separate item is written on its own card, often by alphabet, number system, etc. Hence, such a system or method used to "instruct" or "think" with, one that rotely memorizes or categorizes data without conceptual understanding or the ability to differentiate or associate. Page 115.

finishing touches: final details or actions completing and enhancing a piece of work, etc. Page 11.

first place, in the: 1. firstly; first in order; used to give a fact or reason of primary importance that proves or strengthens what is being stated. Page 4.
2. in or from the beginning; at the outset. Page 65.

five- or twenty-dial drop: a *drop* is the movement of the needle on the E-Meter to the right as one faces it. A drop of five or twenty dials would mean that the needle kept falling a full dial each of the five or twenty times the Tone Arm was moved to bring the needle back on the dial, indicating something is very heavily charged. Page 43.

flattens: knocks down as if with a heavy blow; defeats utterly; completely overwhelms. Page 109.

flicked: moved as if with a quick, sharp jerk. Page 112.

flow: a transfer of energy from one point to another. Page 71.

flows, in all (the): a *flow* is a transfer of energy from one point to another. Auditing in all flows includes *as happening to the preclear, the preclear making it happen to another,* and *as being directed by another at others.* The complete description of flows is contained in *Scientology 8-80.* Page 146.

Fly-Trap: an incident on the theta line. Described in Chapter Nine. Page 115.

force screen: a big heavy force field—which actually is nothing more or less than wave emanation like you get out of a headlight of a car. You change the wavelength of a headlight of a car and speed it up enough and hit somebody with it and it will knock him down. That is an electronic field. That is a force screen. Page 109.

forecast: be able to tell about something in advance of its occurrence; estimate; predict. Page 29.

foregoing: previously written or occurring. Page 23.

foreign tongue: *tongue* means a language of a particular people, region or nation. *Foreign tongue* means a language not of the person or persons being referenced. Page 4.

for his own good: said to someone as if what is being done to them is supposedly helpful or for their benefit, when in fact it is being done out of self-interest or in an effort to punish or dominate, as when a mother, while whipping her screaming child, says, "This is for your own good." Page 116.

forsook: abandoned, departed or withdrew from. Page 131.

for yet a while: for a period of time; still. (*Still* means continuously up to some specified time.) Page 75.

found, will be: will be discovered or known, as through observation of data, research, etc., as in *"will be found to have arrived."* Page 56.

fourth dimension: an imagined dimension employed by physicists in mathematical calculations in an attempt to account for phenomena of space and time they cannot explain within the three dimensions of length, width and depth. Page 73.

Fourth Invader: the fourth of six invader forces into the material universe in the past sixty-four trillion years. *See also* **invader**. Page 104.

fraction: a very small part or segment of something. Page 28.

Frankenstein's monster: a monster created in the book *Frankenstein* by English author Mary Shelley. The title character, Dr. Victor Frankenstein, creates a monster from parts of dead bodies and brings it to life by the power of electricity. Page 65.

freakish: extremely unusual or oddly different from what is normal. Page 52.

French-English conquest of India: a reference to French and British conflicts in India during the eighteenth century for control of coastal land in the eastern part of the country. Page 38.

Freud: (1856–1939) Austrian founder of psychoanalysis who emphasized that unconscious memories of a sexual nature control a person's behavior. Page 101.

frowned down: driven or forced into domination, defeat or disgrace by a look expressive of disapproval or condemnation. Page 106.

full on: completely as possible; totally. Page 128.

full play, in: in full action or operation. Page 29.

funny bone: the popular name for that part of the elbow where a nerve passes between two bones. When struck, it produces a distinct and peculiar tingling sensation in the arm and hand. Page 39.

fuse: to unite or blend into a whole, as if by melting together. Page 107.

gene(s): the basic physical unit of heredity that determines a particular characteristic in an organism and can exist in a number of different forms. Page 38.

genetic: of, pertaining to, or produced by *genes*, the basic unit in the body capable of transmitting characteristics from one generation to the next. Page 12.

genetic being: same as GE as described in Chapter Four. Page 27.

genetic line: the evolutionary chain on Earth. It consists of the total of incidents which have occurred during the evolution of the MEST body itself. The genetic line is described in Chapter Four. Page 12.

genius: the prevailing or distinctive character, power or spirit, such as of a period of time. Page 29.

gifted: possessed of or furnished with. Page 38.

given to: inclined to something or likely to do or be something; having a tendency, as in *"given to chattering"* or *"given to asthma."* Page 88.

go right on: *go on* means to continue doing something; *right* is used for emphasis; hence, *go right on* means to continue along in doing something. Page 65.

gratuitously: given, done or obtained without charge or payment. Page 105.

Greek: shortening of the phrase *it's all Greek to me,* meaning that one cannot understand something, Greek being based on a different alphabet, etc. Page 1.

grief charge: an outburst of tears that may continue for a considerable time. Page 48.

Grim Weeper: a humorous allusion to the *Grim Reaper,* the name given to a skeleton figure representing Death in stories and literature. He is shown in pictures in a long black cloak, which also covers his head, carrying a large scythe (a tool for cutting crops). Death is so called because it is grim (relentlessly harsh) and a reaper (literally, one who cuts and collects a crop such as grain—in this case, people). Page 49.

grotto: a small cave, usually near water and often flooded or liable to flood at high tide. Page 46.

grueling: extremely demanding; thorough and complete. Page 23.

guerrillas: members of a military unit, usually belonging to the area under attack and operating in small, mobile bands in occupied territory to harass and undermine the enemy, as by surprise raids. Page 105.

habit patterns: patterns of behavior created by *habit*, the natural or instinctive tendencies or practices that are characteristic (such as genetically) of particular kinds of plants or animals. Page 4.

halt, the: persons who walk with a limp or uneven step, usually due to some defect or injury. Page 75.

Halver: an incident on the theta line. Described in Chapter Nine. Page 101.

hang up: halt or suspend in progress. Page 85.

hang-up: a suspending from a hook or rail. Hence, *"hang-up in the Weeper"* refers to the condition of being suspended or halted in an incident. Page 48.

harbor: a place of shelter, security, protection, comfort, etc. Page 22.

harboring: giving a place of shelter, security, protection, comfort, etc., to someone or something. Page 21.

hard-eyed: extremely critical and often skeptical. Page 7.

hardly: in a hard manner, with energy, force or strenuous exertion; vigorously. Page 3.

hardwood: the hard, compact, heavy wood of various trees, as the oak or maple, as opposed to *softwood*, such as pine, which is relatively soft. Page 86.

harmonic: used to describe a frequency (number of vibrations per second) which is a multiple of a "fundamental" frequency. If one stretches a string or rubber band and strikes it, a tone or note is produced. One can measure the number of times per second that string is vibrating. Another string, vibrating at certain but different multiples of that vibration rate will sound pleasing. This is calculated out mathematically such as 1, $1/2$, $1/3$, $1/4$, etc. Such can be seen with strings in a piano, each one different in length and vibrating at different rates per second. By striking two or more at a time simultaneously, one can hear which notes are harmonious (pleasing) when played together and which are disharmonious (harsh or not pleasing). Thus, by extension, something which repeats characteristics at a higher or lower point on a scale will be harmonic and seem to be similar and agreeable. Page 85.

Hearst weeklies: a reference to the newspapers and magazines produced by the Hearst Corporation, a large publisher in the US. William Randolph Hearst built the company, achieving unprecedented circulation of his newspapers by the use of many illustrations, color magazine sections, glaring headlines and sensationalistic reporting. Page 74.

heavy facsimile(s): used to be known as an "engram." In view of the fact that it has been found to be stored elsewhere than in the cells, the term "heavy facsimile" has now come into use. A heavy facsimile is an experience, complete with all perceptions and emotions and thoughts and efforts, occupying a precise place in space and a moment in time. It can be an operation, an injury, a term of heavy physical exertion or even a death. It is composed of the preclear's own effort and the effort of the environment (counter-effort); a heavy facsimile is one containing a great deal of thought, emotion, effort or pain. See *Advanced Procedure and Axioms* and *Electropsychometric Auditing* contained in the *Technique 88: Incidents on the Track Before Earth* lecture series package supplement. Page 86.

held back: hesitated in taking some action; were slow or unwilling to do something. Page 5.

Helper: an incident on the genetic line. Described in Chapter Four. Page 39.

"helpful hands": aid; assistance. Used ironically in reference to the between-lives forgetter implants. Page 27.

herald(s): an official messenger and representative of a king or leader in former times. Hence, someone or something performing a similar function. Page 28.

hilt, to the: to the furthest degree possible; completely, thoroughly. A *hilt* is the handle of a sword. Page 116.

hitherto: up to this time, until now. Page 37.

hocus-pocus: unnecessarily mysterious or elaborate activity or talk to cover up a deception, magnify or complicate something simple, etc. Page 104.

holds: maintains as a belief, point of view, etc. Page 39.

Home Universe: a universe a thetan and several others, or just himself, built. Page 80.

Homo novis: new man; from the Latin words *homo* (man) and *novus* (new). Page 62.

hoops, through the: subjected to a rigorous trial or examination. This phrase alludes to circus animals being trained to jump through hoops. Page 98.

horn-rimmed glasses: glasses with frames (rims) made of horn or a substance resembling this. *Horn* is the hard, durable and partly transparent material that tortoiseshells, horses' hooves and similar items are made of. *Horn-rimmed glasses* have frames that are characteristically thicker than other glasses and often black in color. Page 105.

"hot papa" suit: protective apparel worn by a person on an aircraft carrier whose duty is to rescue people from any burning aircraft on the ship's flight deck. Page 105.

How to Audit: the book, *Scientology 8-80*. Page 90.

hung-up: halted or snagged. Page 121.

hydrogen balloons: a reference to balloons filled with *hydrogen*, a gaseous chemical element. Being much lighter than air, hydrogen was sometimes used to fill balloons so that they would rise up in the air. Page 21.

hypnotic: 1. of or having the nature of *hypnosis*, an artificially induced trance state resembling sleep, characterized by a heightened susceptibility to suggestion. Page 53.
2. of or relating to hypnotism. *Hypnotism* is the relaxing or coaxing of a subject into quiescence (a state of rest, quiet, stillness, inactivity or motionlessness). The operator, or hypnotist, then makes certain suggestions to the subject and the subject may, during the session or after it is dictated, obey. Hypnotism is the primary control tool that has been used for the last 76 trillion years. Page 111.

identification tags: either of two oblong metal tags worn suspended around the neck by a member of the armed forces and stamped with his or her name, serial number and other information. Hence, things which serve to identify or give information about someone or something. Page 22.

ill will that blows: evil or hostile feeling or intention (ill will) that happens to come along, bringing misfortune to anyone it strikes.

The phrase alludes to the idea of an *ill wind that blows,* a force that brings misfortune or disaster. *Wind* in this sense means a force, influence or tendency that drives or carries something along, or to which one is exposed. Page 62.

impetuous: moving with great force; violent. Page 48.

implant(s): an idea, belief, desire, command or the like, fixed or instilled deeply in a person's mind or consciousness as through force, pain, etc. Page 103.

inaccessible band: cases at 2.0 or below (on the Tone Scale) which are inaccessible by the auditor. To get a fair measure of accessibility, we find out: Is he in touch with reality? Is he capable of real communication? That a person will close his eyes and go down the track is no sign he is in touch with his past. Page 5.

incident: the recording of an experience, simple or complex, related by the same subject, location or people, understood to take place in a short and finite time period such as minutes or hours or days. Page 5.

Individual Track Map: a book containing charts showing an auditor what to audit and how to chart a preclear's progress. *Track* here refers to a preclear's whole time track. The *Individual Track Map* is contained in the *Technique 88: Incidents on the Track Before Earth* lecture series package supplement. Page 11.

in evidence: actually present; plainly visible; easily seen or noticed. Page 43.

inexhaustible: that cannot be entirely used up; everlasting. Page 20.

inextricable: the condition in which things are so closely linked that they cannot be considered separately and are impossible to get free from. Page 21.

inhibitive: suppressing, restraining or discouraging activity. Page 22.

injected: introduced or added into something. Page 19.

injunctions: commands, directives or orders. Page 63.

in lieu of: in place of; instead of. Page 63.

in order to: as a means to; with the purpose of. Page 48.

in plain view: easily seen or noticed; clearly visible. Page 27.

in-scan: a processing technique whereby the preclear scans feelings of things coming in to him from the environment, the environment putting in things to him, energy manifestations in the incident as they flow in toward the preclear. Page 138.

installation(s): 1. any more or less permanent post, camp, station, base, or the like, for the support or carrying on of military activities. Page 104.
2. something installed; literally, a complete mechanical system fixed in position for use. Used figuratively. Page 108.

intents and purposes, to all: for all practical purposes; practically speaking. Page 11.

in the bulk: in the majority or greater part of something. Page 75.

in the way of: of the nature of; in the matter of; as regards. Page 85.

intimate: involving very close connection or association. Page 53.

invader: reference to invader forces, an electronics people. The electronics people usually happen to be an evolutionary line which is on heavy gravity planets, and so they develop electronics. The reason you say invader forces at all is because at some time fairly early in their youth, they took off to conquer the whole MEST universe. Page 98.

invalidated: a precise definition of invalidation is simply this: It's the statement: "You and your conclusions are wrong." Page 5.

iron maiden: a medieval instrument of torture consisting of an iron frame in human form hinged to admit a victim who was pierced by the spiked interior as the frame closed. Page 145.

jellyfish: any of numerous free-swimming marine animals, characteristically having a gelatinous umbrellalike body and long trailing tentacles. Page 45.

jumps, over the: through a course (as one followed in a cross-country horse race) that presents various obstacles or difficulties, as in riding a horse over a series of barriers or jumps. Page 98.

knocking out: removing forcibly or getting rid of; eliminating. Page 74.

knock out: to eliminate or get rid of. Page 80.

knockout: that makes unconscious. Page 29.

laid down: delivered. Page 103.

lame, the: persons who are crippled through injury to, or defect in, a limb. Page 3.

last-ditch: done finally in desperation to avoid defeat, failure, etc. Page 91.

Lat.: short for *latitude,* the distance measured in degrees of angle of a point on the Earth's surface north or south of the equator. The North Pole is 90 degrees north, the South Pole is 90 degrees south (of the equator). Page 38.

laying in: causing to be positioned, placed or deposited, as if within something. Page 104.

lays in: puts in place or position (as for action or operation). Page 101.

least, at (the) (very): used to add a positive comment about a situation that could be negative, or to mean, even if nothing else is true or one does nothing else, as in *"Here, at the very least, is the explanation," "volcanoes which, at the least, were spectacular," "being able to at least assist the survival."* Page 41.

least, the very: the lowest possible in consideration, rank or importance, as in *"the very least laws of MEST."* Page 63.

legislative passports: a *passport* is a legal document that allows someone the right or privilege to enter into or be active in a certain field or area. *Legislative* means brought about or enforced by the laws (approved by a governmental body). Hence, *legislative passports* refers to having the legal approval, and hence the funding and support, of the government. Page 89.

let sleeping sapiens snore: an allusion to the saying *let sleeping dogs lie,* meaning to avoid interfering in a situation that is currently causing no trouble but might do so as a result of such interference. Page 75.

lie detector: a device used to determine changes in certain body activities, as blood pressure, pulse, breathing and perspiration, the results of which may be interpreted to indicate the truth or falsity of a person's answers under questioning by the police, etc. Page 6.

lies (in): is found; consists or is based on (usually followed by *in*). Page 45.

life continuum: the phenomenon of an individual's tendency to carry on the fears, goals, habits and manifestations of others who have failed, departed or are dead. See *Handbook for Preclears* and its companion lecture series *The Life Continuum.*

lifer: a person sentenced to or serving a term of life imprisonment. Page 7.

light, bring (something) to: make something widely known or evident; reveal or publish something. Page 89.

like of which, the: a person or thing similar to or of the same kind (often used for emphasis). Page 121.

line(s): a continuous series of things, such as incidents, in chronological succession. Page 12.

lobe(s): a rounded projection or subdivision of an organ of the body. Page 40.

Long.: short for *longitude,* the distance measured in degrees of angle of a point on the Earth's surface east or west of a line that runs from the North Pole to the South Pole through Greenwich, England. A circle is 360 degrees—lines of longitude run from 0 to 180 degrees east (E) and from 0 to 180 degrees west (W). Page 38.

long run, in the: after a very lengthy period of time. Page 147.

long since: for a long time; long ago. Page 109.

loose on, turned: given freedom to do something (in order to achieve a particular result). Page 6.

low to high: low tone level to high tone level. Page 92.

Lucretius: (ca. 98–55 B.C.) Roman poet and author of the unfinished instructional poem in six books, *On the Nature of Things,* which set forth in outline a complete science of the universe. Lucretius believed everything, even the soul, is made up of atoms controlled by natural laws. Page 43.

Lysenko: Trofim Denisovich Lysenko (1898–1976), Russian agricultural scientist and biologist of the former Soviet Union. He believed the environment controlled life and attempted to apply Darwin's theories of evolution to agriculture. He was a favorite of Stalin and his theories that negated Man were taught in all Russian schools. Page 41.

made up of: composed of; formed or put together from. Page 17.

magnitude: relative size, amount, scope, importance, extent or influence. Page 81.

magnitude, order of: an arrangement of items in the sequence of their relative size, amount or dimension. *Order* is the sequence or arrangement of things. *Magnitude* is quantity or greatness of size, extent or dimension. Page 18.

make it: to be successful in achieving the specific goal or object referenced. Page 74.

makeshifts: temporary substitutes of an inferior kind. Page 63.

malaction: a bad or wrong action. Page 52.

malcoordination(s): an instance of, or a condition when, a person is not able to move parts of the body smoothly, in harmony or at the same time. Page 40.

malformations: faults and departures from the normal shape, form or structure in a part of the body. Page 19.

malignant: (of a tumor) characterized by uncontrolled growth. Page 31.

Man: the human race or species, humankind, Mankind. Page 3.

man: a human being, without regard to sex or age; a person. Page 52.

manhood: the condition of being a human being. Page 52.

Man off Earth: a reference to the technological advances that enable Man to travel off the planet and into space. Page 6.

marked: significant or noticeable. Page 147.

masochism: enjoyment from pain or degradation inflicted on oneself either as a result of one's own actions or the actions of others, especially the tendency to seek this. Page 50.

mass of twine: *twine*, a strong string or cord made of two or more threads twisted together. A *mass of twine* is a cluster of tangled twine which is difficult to unravel. Page 17.

mastered: conquered or overcome; brought under control. From the original meaning of *master*, a man having control or authority. Page 11.

materially: to a great extent; substantially; considerably. Page 28.

Mathison: the E-Meter in use in 1951, named for Dianeticist, Volney Mathison who built it. Page 5.

maybe: in any engram there is a maybe, two choices, which are relatively evenly balanced. Their even balancing makes an irresolution. The one thing holding up beingness is indecision—a maybe. The anatomy of maybe is covered in the lecture series *The Route to Infinity*. Page 11.

meanest: lowest in quality, character or dignity. Page 65.

mechanical: pertaining to matter, physical forces, etc. Page 1.

mechanical process: a process whose action can be explained by the assumption of mechanical action. Page 1.

mensuration: the act or process of measuring. Page 6.

MEST Clear: an individual who no longer retains engrams or locks. Page 1.

migration(s): (of a cell, tissue, etc.) the act of moving from one area of the body to another. Page 18.

miracle-level: a *level* is relative position or rank on a scale of things; an extent or degree of achievement. *"Miracle-level results"* refers to the outcome (result) of a particular action that ranks as extraordinary or seemingly beyond human power, capable of producing what people generally call a miracle. Page 5.

mirror: reflect in the manner of a mirror (a polished surface which reflects images of objects). Hence, copy or imitate something. Page 20.

misadventures: accidents or other unfortunate or unlucky events. *Mis* means bad or wrong. Page 49.

mischief: harm or trouble; damage or injury usually caused by a specific person or thing. Page 20.

mis-emotionalism: the action or conduct of being mis-emotional. *Mis-* means mistaken, wrong, incorrect. To say that a person was *mis*-emotional would indicate that the person did not display the emotion called for by the actual circumstances of the situation. Being mis-emotional would be synonymous with being irrational. *See also* **counter-mis-emotionalism**. Page 91.

mitosis: the process by which a cell divides into two cells. Page 31.

mock-up: a *mock-up* is something you make which you know is yours and know that you made. You create an illusion—not a facsimile—that approximates a situation, and you then change it in a couple of places in order to solve the problem. Page 71.

modifier(s): something that slightly limits, restricts or changes something else. Page 21.

molars: large back teeth in humans for chewing and grinding. Page 42.

mollusk: an animal with no backbone and a soft body, often having two shells joined by a hinge, such as an oyster or clam. As covered in

Handbook for Preclears, the mollusk marked a stage of the evolutionary line: "First there was a physical universe, which happened we know not how. And then with the cooling planets, there appeared in the seas a speck of living matter. That speck became, eventually, the complicated but still microscopic monocell. And then as the eons passed, it became vegetable matter. And then it became jellyfish. And then it became a mollusk and made its transition into crustaceans. And then as a land animal, this particular track of life which became Man evolved into more and more complex forms: the tarsus, the sloth, the anthropoid and finally Man. There were many intermediate steps." *See also* **anthropoid, crustacean, sloth** and **tarsus.** Page 39.

molten: so hot as to cause metals and other substances (such as rock) to liquefy. Page 63.

monkeyism: monkeylike nature or character; behavior characteristic of a monkey. Page 98.

Motivator: the running of motivators in auditing. Page 61.

motivator: 1. an incident which happens to the preclear and which he dramatizes. See Chapter Ten.
2. an incident which happens to the preclear that he uses to justify committing an overt act. Page 17.
3. the first basic injury is called the motivator; the injury to the individual himself. So called because it motivates his later dramatization. When he commits an overt act there may show up upon his body the bruises he inflicted on his victim. Only they're not transferred from the victim: they come out of the motivator. Page 29.

motor: of, pertaining to or involving muscular movement. Page 22.

much less: used to characterize a statement or suggestion as still more unacceptable than one that has been already denied; and certainly not. Page 61.

much to (one's) surprise: used to express that someone is extremely amazed or in wonder, disbelief or the like, at some occurrence. Page 81.

mumbo jumbo: language or ritualistic activity intended to confuse. Also obscure or meaningless talk or writing; nonsense. Page 98.

mutation, electronic: *mutation* is a random change in the hereditary material of an organism's cells resulting in a new trait or characteristic, as distinguished from a variation resulting from generations of gradual change. Various influences can cause the hereditary material to change, one of which can be electronic particles whether from direct contact of the body or through beams or rays. This change is then passed on to the organism's offspring. Page 38.

mystic(s): a person who claims to attain, or believes in the possibility of attaining, insight into mysteries transcending ordinary human knowledge, as by direct communication with the divine or immediate intuition in a state of spiritual ecstasy. Page 97.

mysticism: the belief that it is possible to achieve knowledge of spiritual truths and God through contemplation or through meditation. Page 97.

natural selection: the process by which forms of life having traits that better enable them to adapt to specific environmental pressures, such as predators, changes in climate, competition for food or mates, will tend to survive and reproduce in greater numbers than others of their kind, thus ensuring the perpetuation of those favorable traits in succeeding generations. A *predator* is an animal that hunts, kills and eats other animals in order to survive, or any other organism that behaves in a similar manner. Page 38.

nerve system: a network of pathways by which certain kinds of information travel throughout the body. The system functions by receiving signals from all parts of the body, relaying them to the brain and spinal cord, and then sending appropriate return signals to muscles and body organs so that the body can respond to the information. Page 39.

neurotic: a person who is struggling to combat the present. He has not given up the strain of keeping some of his attention in present time, and will not do so until forced by a chronic, constant restimulation to do so. The neurotic is interested and concerned with the present, and the sane is interested in the future. Page 33.

new cult: a reference to early Christianity which emerged in the midst of older established religions with the belief that God had created the world and created Man from the dust of Earth and all animals from the ground. During the first five hundred years after Christ and before the birth of the prophet Mohammed (founder of Islam), missionaries spread Christianity eastward across the old Persian Empire (30° to 80° East Longitude, 30° North Latitude). Page 38.

Nipping: nipping is fully described in Chapter Nine, section on "Nipping." Page 81.

Nirvana: the goal of the Hindus. Hindu beliefs are that "Reality is One" (Brahma) and that ultimate salvation, and release from the endless cycle of birth to death, is achieved when one merges or is absorbed into the "one divine reality," with all loss of individual existence. Hence the phrase *join Nirvana*. Page 97.

nitrous oxide: a sweet-smelling, sweet-tasting gas used in dentistry and surgery to render the patient unconscious. Page 112.

Noah: Biblical character instructed by God to build an ark (large rudderless ship) for his wife and family and a pair of each of Earth's animals. God, resolving to destroy the wickedness of people, then flooded Earth with forty days and forty nights of rain, drowning all living creatures. When the rain ceased and the water drained, Noah and the others began a new life on Earth.

no matter: it is of no consequence or importance; it makes no difference; regardless of. Page 17.

noteworthy: deserving notice or attention; interesting. Page 5.

now and then: occasionally; sometimes; from time to time. Page 4.

nuclear physicist: a specialist in the field of *nuclear physics*, that branch of physics that deals with the behavior, structure and component parts of the center of an atom (called a nucleus), which makes up almost all of the mass of the atom. Page 87.

nuclear physics: the branch of physics that deals with the behavior, structure and component parts of the center of an atom (called the nucleus), which makes up almost all of the mass of the atom. Page 87.

number of, to the: at the quantity or amount of. Page 29.

obscurity: the condition of being unknown; not obvious. Page 28.

occasioned: brought about, caused. Page 22.

occluded: having memories shut off from one's awareness; from *occlude*, to close, shut or stop up (a passage, opening, etc.). Page 48.

odds, against considerable: variation of *against all odds*, meaning despite the great probability that what one wants or hopes for does not exist or will not occur. Page 3.

old-time: of, relating to or characteristic of a time in the past and specifically in this sense, Dianetic auditing from 1950 to 1951, as in *"Old-time incidents were said to go into recession."* Page 85.

once and for all: finally and for the last time; permanently. Page 133.

on record: existing and set down in some preserved form and available for viewing such as by the public, as in *"Pre-ovum sequences are on record, but are not common."* Page 31.

onslaught: the energetic and vigorous undertaking of some action likened to a strong or forceful attack. Page 7.

operator(s): one who controls the functioning of a machine or other equipment. Page 7.

order: a group or kind having rank in a scale of quality or importance, or distinguished from others by nature or character. Page 146.

order of magnitude: an arrangement of items in the sequence of their relative size, amount or dimension. *Order* is the sequence or arrangement of things. *Magnitude* is quantity or greatness of size, extent or dimension. Page 18.

ornate: having heavy, elaborate or excessive decoration. Page 113.

outlook, takes a poor: has a low opinion of something; views or regards something with an unfavorable attitude. Page 56.

out of: arising from; from a base or grounding in. Said of something nonmaterial. Page 4.

outpulse: a short burst of radiated energy that moves outward and away from the source. Page 111.

outraged: greatly offended or shocked (against some idea or view held of how something should be). Page 23.

outright: without reservation or limit; openly. Page 40.

out-scan: a processing technique whereby the preclear scans feelings of outflow from himself into the environment, what he injected into the environment, the energy emanating from the preclear to the environment in the incident. Page 138.

outsoar: to soar above or beyond. Used figuratively to indicate going way above or beyond. Page 90.

overlord: to rule or govern domineeringly. An *overlord* is one having power or supremacy over other lords and people. During the Middle Ages (400s to 1400s) a *lord* was a powerful landowner to whom service and obedience were owed. Page 62.

Overt: the running of overt acts in auditing. Page 61.

Overt Act(s): refers to the auditing approach to overt acts to address the overt act phenomenon. *See* **overt act**. Page 86.

overt act: 1. an incident which the preclear does to another dynamic. See Chapter Ten. Page 5.

2. something harmful a preclear has done to another, as opposed to what has been done to him by another. Page 29.

3. the overt act phenomenon: *"that pain which you render on any other dynamic will be mirrored in yourself."* The individual will actually fall under the control center of a person he has damaged by an overt act. If you injure a dynamic badly, you have a definite commitment with yourself to continue the existence of that dynamic. That's the overt act and life continuum. *See also* **life continuum**. Page 146.

overt and motivator invalidations: invalidation is any thought, emotion or effort, counter-thought, counter-emotion or counter-effort which denies or smothers the thought, emotion or effort of the individual. Overt invalidations would be those invalidations which the preclear does to another dynamic. Motivator invalidations would be those invalidations which happen to the preclear and which he dramatizes. Page 91.

ovum: a female reproductive cell. Page 29.

"packed in": brought or put closely together with other things in order to, or as if to, become formed into a compact body; crowded together. Page 107.

pack instincts: a *pack* is a group of animals, such as dogs or wolves, that run and hunt together. An *instinct* is an inborn pattern of behavior characteristic of a species and shaped by biological necessities such as survival and reproduction. *Pack instinct* therefore is the inborn pattern of behavior of a group of men or animals that run and hunt together, such as attacking prey, defense, etc. Page 52.

palls: coverings that darken or obscure, such as clouds that extend over a thing or region and produce an effect of gloom. Page 49.

paradoxes: people, situations, acts, etc., that seem to have contradictory or inconsistent qualities. From a Greek word which means contrary to expectation, incredible. Page 66.

parity: the state or condition of being equal, or on a level with as in amount, status or character. Page 146.

part and parcel: an essential, necessary or integral part. Page 92.

part of, on the: regarding or with respect to the person or thing that is specified. Page 6.

pass out: to become unconscious. Page 73.

patron saints: those who are looked upon as special guardians of a person, place, country, institution, group, etc. Used humorously. Page 41.

pawn: an object kept as security against something else such as when borrowing money. Page 107.

pawn, body in: a body held in one place, hypnotized or knocked out, where the person is told that he belongs *here,* but he must go over *here* and live. The body is floating in fluid or under a constant electronic bath. They're lying on a pallet or something of the sort; the body is completely motionless. He's just nebulously monitored by that body, because somebody can walk in, stir up the body, give the body a command, and he himself will perceive the command. Described in the lecture series *Technique 88: Incidents on the Track Before Earth.* See also Chapter Nine, section on "The Double-Body." Page 107.

perilously: in a condition or manner that is full of grave risk; dangerously. Page 48.

Persia: an ancient and vast empire (mid-500s B.C. to mid-A.D. 600s), located in western and southwestern Asia that included parts of what are now Iran and Afghanistan. Beginning around 550 B.C., Persia was greatly expanded into a vast empire, conquering neighboring kingdoms throughout the Middle East, including Babylonia and Egypt, and eventually became the most powerful state in the world. Page 41.

pervaded: passed or spread throughout all parts. Page 41.

pervading: spreading through or into every part of. Page 71.

pervasion: a method of knowing by casting one's beingness a sufficient distance to pervade (spread through or into every part of) some subject. Pervasion is described in the lecture series *Technique 88: Incidents on the Track Before Earth.* Page 71.

Phoenicia: an ancient kingdom located in what is now roughly Syria, Lebanon and Israel. Page 41.

phonograph-record-like: in the manner of a *phonograph record,* a vinyl (plastic) disc (normally 12 inches in diameter) with grooves (indentations) in it, on which music, voice or other sounds are recorded and which can be played over and over again. Page 29.

photon: a unit particle of light. Just as matter is composed of atoms, light is composed of photons. Page 39.

Photon Converter: an incident on the genetic line. Described in Chapter Four. Page 39.

physicist: a scientist who specializes in *physics,* the science that deals with matter, energy, motion and force, including what these things are, why they behave as they do and the relationship between them, as contrasted to the life sciences such as biology, which studies and observes living organisms such as animals and plants. Page 43.

physioelectrical: concerning the electricity relating to or of living things. Page 6.

pick(ed)(s) up: 1. acquire as knowledge, as in *"Darwin and his co-workers picked up this theory after the Vedic Hymns had been transplanted to Europe."* Page 38.
2. to bring into range and receive, as in *"It takes a radio set to pick up or contact this field strongly enough to get a good reaction out of it."* Page 87.
3. to take hold of, as in *"A high-scale thetan can pick up and discard facsimiles at will."* Page 100.
4. take into custody; seize or capture, as in *"The new crew in the area is later quite surprised to find that their planted beings, so carefully dumped in the sea from a saucer, are being picked up between-lives and given 'treatment' by an old, established invader."* Page 109.
5. to obtain, as in *"Thereafter, every time any energy flows through this thetan on the post, the post picks up the energy and flows it back up inside him."* Page 146.

pictures of champions: a reference to the pictures of the best or great sportsmen on *trading cards,* small cards depicting professional athletes, collected, cherished and traded, especially by children. Page 79.

piker: something done in a small, weak and poor way; a faint, inaccurate indication of something else, as in *"Modern science fiction, even that, is a weak piker compared to the data of the past from which these writers of the future took their plots."* Page 90.

Piltdown Man: the remains of apelike bones found in the town of Piltdown, England, in 1912, alleged at the time to be those of a primitive form of human being and thought to be a missing evolutionary link between apes and early human bodies. Page 52.

pineal: the pineal gland, a small cone-shaped endocrine gland located in the brain. It secretes a hormone important in the regulation of biological cycles such as blood pressure and body temperature. Page 104.

pinned down: held fast in a spot so that one cannot get away; held down or against something by force. Page 72.

pituitary: the pituitary gland, a small oval gland at the base of the brain. It produces hormones that control other glands and influence growth of bone structure, sexual maturing and general metabolism. Page 104.

plain view, in: easily seen or noticed; clearly visible. Page 27.

plankton: a mass of tiny animals and plants floating in the sea, usually near the surface. Page 44.

Plato: (ca. 427–347 B.C.) Greek philosopher and teacher who stated people sometimes do not seek to be virtuous as they do not realize that virtue produces happiness, and that immoral behavior is the symptom of a diseased soul. Page 66.

played over: aimed, directed, or fired, sometimes continuously so as to strike, move or pass over. Page 104.

plot out: to lay out or show the process, condition or course of something, as if with the precision used to chart the course of a ship, draw a map of an area, etc. Page 80.

pneumatic drills: large, powerful tools, driven by air pressure, used especially for breaking up road surfaces. *Pneumatic* comes from Greek *pneuma* meaning wind or air, and a *drill* is a cutting tool for making holes in something. The rapid-fire, back-and-forth motion of the drill drives it down into the material. Prolonged use is considered dangerous to the operator (usually a man), thus it is often referred to as a "widow-maker." Page 105.

poise: self-possession; steadiness or stability. Page 29.

populace: all the people in a given area; population. Page 116.

post: a type of theta trap. Posts are described in the Supplement, section under "Theta Trap Posts." Page 88.

potpourri: any mixture, especially of unrelated objects, subjects, etc. Page 64.

practice of, made a: did (something) regularly and frequently. Page 5.

prankish: done as a mischievous trick. Page 72.

210

preconception: the period of time prior to *conception*, the fertilization of an egg by a sperm at the beginning of pregnancy. Page 12.

prenatal: a Dianetic term used to denote experience and incidents which take place and are recorded in the mind while in the womb prior to or during birth. Page 5.

presupposes: believes or assumes beforehand or in advance; expects. Page 11.

Preventive Dianetics: that branch of Dianetics that has as its basis the prevention of acquisition of an engram; secondarily, when an engram has been received in spite of all due care and caution, the prevention of restimulation of the engram. Page 29.

prey to: someone who is vulnerable to, or a victim of, something hostile or injurious. Page 62.

probabilities: the chances or possibilities of something happening. Page 6.

profit: advantage; benefit; gain; progress made. Page 17.

prone: 1. have a natural tendency to something. Page 30.
2. inclined to be affected by something; likely to experience something. Page 123.

proportion, out of: larger, more serious, important, etc., in relation to something, than is necessary or appropriate; having no appropriate relation in size, amount, importance, etc. Page 28.

protoplasm: jellylike liquid that is present in the cells of all living plants, animals and humans and consists of the living matter of plant and animal cells. Page 29.

protoplasmic line: pertaining to the protoplasm line. Page 28.

protoplasm line: the evolution of organisms themselves, continuing along a protoplasmic line from generation to generation; the conception, birth and growth of bodies; the genetic line and evolutionary chain on Earth. Page 29.

proven-up: finally tested, shown to be successful. *Up* means to or toward a state of completion or finality. Page 103.

psychosomatics: body sensations, pains or discomfort stemming from the mind making the body ill, from *psycho* (mind) and *somatic* (body). The description of the cause and source of psychosomatics is contained in *Dianetics: The Modern Science of Mental Health*. Page 18.

psychotics: individuals who are out of contact to a thorough extent with their present time environment and who do not compute into the future. A psychotic may be an acute psychotic, wherein he becomes psychotic for only a few minutes at a time and only occasionally in certain environments (as in rages or apathies), or he may be a chronic psychotic (or in a continual disconnect with the future and present). Psychotics who are dramatically harmful to others are considered dangerous enough to be put away. Psychotics who are harmful on a less dramatic basis are no less harmful to their environment and are no less psychotic. Page 29.

pugnacious: combative; inclined to fight. Page 51.

pull off: to accomplish or perform successfully, especially something requiring cleverness, or against great odds. Page 74.

pulp: the soft, sensitive tissue in the center of a tooth, including blood vessels, nerves, etc. Page 18.

pummeling: beating or pounding with continuous, repeated blows. Page 104.

purloined: stolen; taken for oneself. Page 79.

put out (one's) eyes: to make someone permanently unable to see, such as by the eyes coming out of their sockets. Page 71.

putting on a show: presenting or performing an impressive or striking appearance or display. Page 74.

Pyrenees: a mountain range in southwestern Europe which forms a natural boundary between France and Spain. Page 110.

quarters: a reference to the four major divisions of the compass; north, south, east and west. Hence *coming from various quarters* means from different locations or directions. Page 28.

quartz stone: *quartz* is a brilliant, crystalline mineral, occurring in abundance, most often in a colorless and transparent form. A *quartz stone* was an early form of magnifying glass. Page 6.

radioactive: relating to the emission (radiating) of energy or particles. *Radio* in this sense means emitting rays. Page 111.

radio set: a device that receives incoming radio signals and converts them to perceptible forms, such as sound. Also called simply a radio. Page 87.

rancor: bitter hate or ill will; resentment. Page 146.

random, at: with no set plan; without method or prior arrangement. Page 4.

rapport: relationship, especially a close or sympathetic relationship or emotional affinity; agreement. Page 53.

razorbacks: a reference to razor clams, any of a variety of burrowing clams having long, narrow, rectangular shells, that resemble the handle of an old-fashioned straight razor. Page 46.

Reader's Digest: a pocket-sized American magazine begun in 1922 which contains reprinted articles condensed from books and other periodicals in a number of fields, such as medicine. Page 5.

rebukes: sharp or severe criticisms or disapprovals. Page 52.

receiving set: a device that receives incoming radio signals and converts them to perceptible forms, such as sound. Also called simply a radio. Page 87.

recession: a condition wherein an incident apparently disappears or simply goes out of sight without being erased. Page 85.

reconcile: to make two or more apparently conflicting things consistent or compatible; bring into agreement or harmony. Page 64.

record(s): 1. a person's (or thing's) accomplishments or performance to date, as in *"Their general record with preclears was very poor."* Page 5. **2.** an account of facts or events preserved in a lasting form, as in *"It has a record, in many cases, of the entire experience forward until the last life."* Page 19. **3.** makes a lasting account of facts or events; preserves the memory of something permanently, as in *"It records every perception present, asleep or awake, conscious or unconscious."* Page 29. **4.** a vinyl (plastic) disc (normally 12 inches in diameter) with grooves (indentations) in it, on which music, voice or other sounds are permanently recorded and which can be played over and over again. Page 29.

recourse to: the act or instance of turning to something for aid, use or help. Page 131.

reduce: become free of aberrative material as far as possible. Page 28.

reflex response: an automatic reaction performed by a part of the body without conscious effort as a result of a nerve impulse. For example, a common reflex point is at the knee and when the muscle of the kneecap is hit lightly, the lower leg gives an involuntary jerk upward (reflex response). Page 39.

register: to appear or produce a response on a recording or measuring instrument. Page 5.

relaxed: calm and not worried or tense. Page 21.

repercussion: a widespread, indirect or unforeseen effect of an act, action or event. Page 5.

report stations: a reference to locations where the thetan "reports in" between lives and receives an implant. Page 110.

Republican: of or related to the Republican Party, one of the two major political parties in the United States originally organized in 1854. Republicans are usually associated with business, financial and some agricultural interests of the US and with favoring a restricted governmental role in social and economic life. Page 98.

residual: present or existing, often with the sense of being a quantity left over at the end of a series of actions, conditions, etc. Page 39.

restimulation: the reactivation of a past incident by the appearance of a similarity to the content of the past incident. Page 12.

retractor screen(s): screens (things that function to shield, protect or conceal), that act as a *retractor,* a wave that can pull back instead of push out. You turn a hose on somebody. This pushes him back. There can exist a wave which, if it were a hose, would pull you up to the nozzle instead of push you away. Thetans can put out such a retractor wave. You have to hang together a solid flow, so to speak, and then make the solid flow collapse in order to get a retractor wave. It's to grab hold of something and hold it and pull it in. Page 113.

revolution: a sudden, complete or radical change of any kind in a condition, situation, subject, field of activity, etc. Page 18.

ridges: ridges are essentially suspended energy in space. A ridge is caused by two energy flows coinciding and causing an enturbulence of energy which on examination is found to take on a characteristic which—in energy flows—is very like matter, having its particles in chaotic mixture. Page 19.

rig up: assemble, set up in order to achieve a particular end. Page 88.

rising tide: *tide* is the periodic rising and falling of the surface level of the oceans or other bodies of water, most noticeable at the shoreline.

Hence, *rising tide* is the inflow of water from the sea in a specific location, such as at the shore, a cave, etc. Page 46.

road, get the show on the: to get (an organization, plan, project, etc.) started, put in motion and operating. This phrase comes from the early 1900s, when acting companies, theaters and circuses would tour all over the country giving shows, and *get the show on the road* literally meant to get the show packed up and traveling on the road to the place(s) it was going to perform. Page 1.

rotogravure section: the magazine section of a newspaper. The term derives from the type of printing press used to print photographs. Page 74.

rule out: exclude something or decide not to consider something. Page 98.

run out: exhaust the negative influence of something; erase. Page 80.

saddling: putting upon (someone) as a burden, obligation, responsibility, etc. A *saddle* is a leather seat for a rider secured to an animal's back. Page 66.

sadistic: gaining pleasure from causing physical or mental pain to others. Page 42.

same, just the: in the same manner; nevertheless; despite a particular situation or comment. Page 87.

sanitarium: an institution for the mentally ill. Page 29.

saucer: flying saucer, a spacecraft that is flat and round, like a disk or saucer (a small shallow, round dish to hold food or a cup). Page 109.

scalloped-lip: having a lip with a wavy outer edge, like the shell of the shellfish known as a scallop. Page 46.

scan: to glance over systematically. *See* **in-scan** and **out-scan**. Page 47.

scathingly: in a manner that is bitterly severe. Page 5.

schools of "thought": a reference to the subjects of modern psychology, psychiatry and psychoanalysis which failed to accurately identify and describe how the mind actually works. *Schools* here means a body of persons that has been taught by or follows a particular authority or teacher and is associated or united by common principles, beliefs, methods, etc. *Thought* in this sense refers to the mind or that which is in the mind. Page 4.

Schopenhauer: Arthur Schopenhauer (1788–1860), German philosopher known for his philosophy of pessimism and who believed that only the cessation of desire can solve the universal impulse of the will to live. Page 64.

score(s): 1. very many. Page 6.
2. twenty of anything such as hours, people, etc. Page 32.

seat: basis or foundation. Page 50.

second-rate: of lesser or minor quality, importance, or the like; inferior; mediocre. Page 62.

semblance: the apparent form of something. Page 37.

sense of: a keen perceptive awareness of or sensitivity to the presence or importance of something. Page 72.

sentient: conscious or capable of perceptions; consciously perceiving. Page 64.

Separation from the Main Body of Theta: the first incident on the whole track. One becomes an individual. He feels like he has been rejected or kicked out. Page 80.

short, in: introducing a summary statement of what has been previously stated in a few words; in summary. Page 17.

short, to be: briefly and plainly; in a few words. Page 23.

show on the road, get the: to get (an organization, plan, project, etc.) started, put in motion and operating. This phrase comes from the early 1900s, when acting companies, theaters and circuses would tour all over the country giving shows, and *get the show on the road* literally meant to get the show packed up and traveling on the road to the place(s) it was going to perform. Page 1.

shows them up: makes something visible; displays in order that it may be looked at, seen, etc.; presents to view. Page 20.

shy of: unwilling or reluctant to do something; fearful of committing oneself to a particular course of action. Page 12.

silicosis: a disease of the lungs caused by the inhaling of dust containing silica (a hard glassy mineral), as by stonecutters. Page 105.

since: ago; before now. Page 37.

skyscraper: figuratively, a very, very high condition or state. A *skyscraper* is a very tall building of many stories (or floors), especially one for office or commercial use. So called because it "scrapes (rubs against) the sky." Page 62.

slipped a cable or two: a variation of *slip one's trolley*, meaning to lose one's sanity or act in a confused mental state; to act irrationally. The phrase refers to a trolley car connected to and powered by an overhead electrical cable. Literally, *to slip one's trolley* means that the trolley slips off the cable and separates the vehicle from its power source. Page 23.

sloth: a slow-moving, tree-dwelling mammal with a fur-covered body, a flat, short head, large eyes and a short nose turned up at the tip. It characteristically hangs, back down, from branches. Page 51.

softened-up: having had one's resistance or opposition broken by physical or mental torture. Page 20.

solar plexus: a mass of nerve cells situated at the upper part of the abdomen, behind the stomach. Page 20.

solar system: the Sun together with all the planets and other bodies that revolve around it. Page 110.

somatic entities: genetic entities. The somatic entity is responsible for having developed the body and has on its file all of the genetic-line data. It is running the body up to the point where the body is joined by the theta being and the other entities. Page 61.

somatic mind: as defined in *Dianetics: The Modern Science of Mental Health,* that mind which, directed by the analytical or reactive mind, places solutions into effect on the physical level. Page 19.

somatics: physical pains or discomforts of any kind. Page 18.

sordidly: of a coarse, gross or inferior character or nature. Page 131.

source-points: places or locations from which waves, flows or the like emanate. Page 99.

specific gravity: the density of a material as compared to the density of water. For instance, the specific gravity of gold is 19.3 because any volume of gold weighs 19.3 times as much as the same volume of water. Page 1.

spirals: plural for *spiral*, a term of lives or a term of existences or a single existence which bear an intimate relation, one to the other. Page 80.

spiritualism: the doctrine or belief that the spirits of the dead can and do communicate with the living, especially through a person (medium). Page 98.

spore: a small, usually one-celled reproductive unit capable of giving rise to a new individual without sexual activity. Page 47.

sprawling: spread out or developed in a disordered or irregular way. Page 38.

squads: many groups of things, people, etc., often engaged in the same activity. Literally, a *squad* is a small number of soldiers (usually about twelve) forming a military unit. Page 45.

squares, three: three nourishing or filling meals a day, that is, breakfast, lunch and dinner. Page 62.

stars: other worlds and locations than Earth. Page 4.

Starter: the action of the theta being joining the track immediately prior to birth. Page 31.

static: fixed and unmoving; without motion. Page 46.

stature(s): importance, quality or status gained by impressive growth, development or achievement; an achieved level. Page 41.

stethoscope: a medical instrument used for listening to breathing, heartbeats and other sounds made by the body. One end of the stethoscope fits into the ears of the person making the observations and the other end of the instrument consists of a flat, disk-shaped device which is placed on the area being listened to. Page 29.

Straightwire: the name of a process. It is the act of stringing a line between present time and some incident in the past, and stringing that line directly and without any detours. The auditor is stringing a straight "wire" of memory between the actual genus (origin) of a condition and present time, thus demonstrating that there is a difference of time and space in the condition then and the condition now, and that the preclear, conceding this difference, then rids himself of the condition or at least is able to handle it. See *Self Analysis*. Page 98.

straw added to the weight of an earlier facsimile hang-up: a reference to the phrase *the straw that broke the camel's back*, the final thing that when added to a bad or unpleasant situation causes failure, ruin, etc. Page 122.

striven: tried very hard; made great efforts (to achieve something). Page 97.

stroke: brain damage caused by a lack of blood flow to part of the brain such as when a blood vessel becomes blocked. A *stroke* results in permanent damage to the brain tissue and may cause paralysis on one or both sides of the body. Page 40.

strung on: (of a series of objects, etc.) put or arranged on string or wire. Page 103.

stuffed like snakes: a reference to the feeding habits of snakes who often go without food for weeks or months and then eat in single, large quantities, swallowing their prey whole. Page 116.

styled: named or called. Page 64.

subjugation: under complete control or domination. Page 40.

subscribing: giving one's support, agreement or approval to some opinion, plan of action or the like. Page 65.

sudden (statements): happening, made or done quickly without warning, or unexpectedly. Page 23.

sulfurous: of or like sulfur, a pale yellow substance that produces a strong unpleasant smell when it burns. Page 49.

sum and total: a combined total of separate components; totality. Page 17.

summons to court: a command likened to a *summons to court,* an authoritative order to appear in court, as before a judge, in order to respond to a charge. Page 104.

superstitions: beliefs, not based on reason or knowledge. Page 3.

suppositions: things assumed to be true (which may be either true or false) as the basis for forming a theory or course of action. Page 18.

surf: the mass of white bubbles formed by waves as they fall upon the shore or the waves themselves as they break upon the shore. Page 44.

sway: prevailing, overpowering or controlling influence. Page 89.

sweep: an extent, range or scope as of thought, observation, experience, etc., likened to what would be encompassed by a wide curving motion. Page 71.

sweetness and syrup: a variation of *sweetness and light,* a phrase referring to an attitude or actions of extreme or excessive kindliness and gentleness. Page 116.

swindling: deceiving or cheating someone. Page 5.

switchboards: boards containing switches and other devices for controlling electric flows and used to connect and disconnect communication lines. Page 39.

Symbological Processing: a book containing a type of processing that employs sixty-eight different symbols that are shown to the preclear by the auditor. The complete title of the book is *A Key to the Unconscious, Symbological Processing* and is contained in the *Technique 88: Incidents on the Track Before Earth* lecture series package supplement. *See also* **symbols, take incidents as he (the auditor) is given them by.** Page 27.

symbols, take incidents as he (the auditor) is given them by: a reference to Symbological Processing, in part of which the person being processed, using a book containing sixty-eight different symbols, tells the auditor what person or object or thing in the real universe, or what circumstance or state of being, the symbol represents. The person being processed then is required to recall an incident involving this person or object or state of being. Page 32.

synthetics: from synthetic—not real or genuine. *Synthetics* are artificial entities that operate entirely on a stimulus-response basis. Page 19.

system: *solar system,* the Sun together with all the planets and other bodies that revolve around it. Page 62.

system, file-card: literally, a highly structured arrangement of information, in which a separate item is written on its own card, often by alphabet, number system, etc. Hence, such a system or method used to "instruct" or "think" with, one that rotely memorizes or categorizes data without conceptual understanding or the ability to differentiate or associate. Page 115.

system, solar: the Sun together with all the planets and other bodies that revolve around it. Page 110.

tab: a tag or label that identifies or gives information about something. Page 100.

tailored: fashioned or formed into (something) as if by a *tailor,* one who makes, alters or repairs clothes. Page 114.

tailor-making: making or adapting for a particular purpose. From the idea of clothes that are *tailor-made,* made by a tailor to particular taste or demand, rather than in a factory. Page 88.

tanglement: the fact or condition of being *tangled,* mixed together or intertwined in a confused mass. Page 21.

tar pits: areas where tar or asphalt naturally accumulates, trapping animals and preserving their bones. Page 38.

tarsus: a reference to a *tarsier,* a small nocturnal (active at night) tree-dwelling mammal with long legs, a short fur-covered body, a rounded head and unusually large eyes.

Technique 8-80: see the book *Scientology 8-80.* Page 147.

Technique 80: the cultivation of disintegration of engrams instead of going over them and over them and over them. Technique 80 doesn't have very much to do with facsimiles or their erasure or running on a time track. One simply disintegrates the engrams. It is a development of that facility. The Technique 80 lectures containing the complete description of this technology are available as *The Route to Infinity.* Page 1.

Technique 88: Technique 88 is processing the theta body, and anything that pertains to processing the theta body can be lumped into it. When we examine Technique 88, we examine whole track. The whole track could not be audited at all until Attention Unit Running and Overt Acts had been developed and refined for auditor application. The tracking of attention units and the skills necessary to that are the requisites in running theta-track incidents. Technique 88 includes the data of where the theta being has been and what it has done. Technique 88 is fully described in the lecture series *Technique 88: Incidents on the Track Before Earth.* See also "A Step-by-Step Breakdown of 88" at the end of the book. Page 1.

teleportation: the act of transporting or being transported across space and distance instantly. Page 73.

tell: reveal or make known to. Page 7.

tenets: any opinions, principles, beliefs, etc., held true by members of a profession, group, etc. Page 38.

tenth-rate: an extension of the term *second-rate,* of lesser or minor quality, importance, or the like; inferior; mediocre. Hence, tenth-rate is distinctly inferior and of even lesser quality. Page 62.

that is that: a phrase showing that something has come to an end, sometimes said of someone's life. Page 111.

that is to say: a phrase used to introduce a clearer, more comprehensible, restatement of what immediately precedes or to limit or modify it. Page 88.

the like of which: a person or thing similar to or of the same kind (often used for emphasis). Page 121.

theory of evolution: the idea that all living things evolved from simple organisms and changed through the ages to produce millions of different species: the theory that development of a species or organism from its original or primitive state to its present state includes adaptation (form or structure modified to better survive and multiply in a changed environment). Page 37.

theosophy: any of various forms of philosophical or religious thought supposedly based on special mystical insight. Page 98.

therein: in that matter, circumstance, thing, etc. Page 45.

theta: the mathematical symbol for the static of thought. By theta is meant the static itself. Page 1.

theta being: the preclear himself, the "I". Page 19.

theta body: the theta beingness; the individual that inhabits the body. Page 12.

theta body line: the collected memories of one individual, the theta being, as opposed to the protoplasm or genetic line. Relationships of these lines are described in Chapter Four. Page 12.

Theta Clear: the thetan cleared of a necessity to have a MEST body. Page 23.

Theta Clearing: bringing a being up to a point where it can leave and return upon a MEST body. Page 1.

thetan: this term designates the beingness of the individual, the awareness of awareness unit, that quantity and identity which *is* the preclear. Page 1.

theta traps: a particular variety of theta-line incidents, as described in Chapter Nine, section on "Theta Traps." Page 98.

the very least: the lowest possible in consideration, rank or importance, as in *"the very least laws of MEST."* Page 63.

they who are about to die: a reference to the statement given by Roman gladiators to the emperor before fighting began at the Roman games, large spectacles in which as many as 300 pairs of gladiators, armed with swords and spears, would fight each other to the death for the entertainment of thousands of spectators. A *gladiator* is a person, usually a professional combatant, a captive, or a slave, trained to entertain the public by engaging in combat to the death with another person or a wild animal in the ancient Roman arena. Page 66.

thin air: literally, air, a gaseous substance that will not support any object. *Thin* means lacking body or substance. Page 111.

30° N. Lat., 30° to 80° E. Long., Earth: a reference to the location of the old Persian Empire. Early Christianity emerged in the midst of older established religions with the belief that God had created the world and created Man from the dust of Earth and all animals from the ground. During the first five hundred years after Christ and before the birth of the prophet Mohammed (founder of Islam), missionaries spread Christianity eastward across the old Persian Empire (30° to 80° East Longitude, 30° North Latitude). Page 38.

thought: the facsimiles one has recorded of his various environments and the facsimiles he has created with his imaginings, their recombination and evaluations and conclusions for the purpose of determining action or no action or potential action or no action. Thought produces motion or action through the medium of emotion. Thought is without time. It is instantaneous. The subject of thought can be found in *Advanced Procedure and Axioms* and its companion lecture series *Thought, Emotion and Effort*. Page 1.

thought police: a police force established to suppress freedom of thought. The concept, and name, first appeared in the science-fiction novel *1984* by English author George Orwell (1903–1950). In *1984*, Orwell describes thought police who arrest, imprison and "re-educate" citizens who are demonstrating unorthodox ideas or rebellion against the government. Page 90.

three actions of energy, the: there are only three actions of energy: it can flow; it can form ridges and it can disperse. The three actions of energy are fully described in the lecture series *Technique 88: Incidents on the Track Before Earth*. Page 11.

threescore and ten: seventy years, viewed as the average length of time a person is likely to live. A *score* here equals twenty years. Page 7.

three squares: three nourishing or filling meals a day, that is, breakfast, lunch and dinner. Page 62.

time-space universes: universes other than the physical universe, containing their own time and space. Page 73.

time stream: time thought of as a continuous flowing progression. Page 73.

time warps: hypothetical distortions in space and time allowing time to stand still or people to travel from one time to another. Page 73.

tolerance band: the range or level (as on a scale) in which something, such as the human body, has the ability and capacity to survive. Page 62.

tome: a book, especially a very heavy, large or learned book. Page 41.

Tone Scale charts: a reference to the Hubbard Chart of Human Evaluation found in *Science of Survival*, the Tone Scale found in *Self Analysis*, and the Chart of Attitudes found in *Handbook for Preclears*. Page 17.

tongue, foreign: *tongue* means a language of a particular people, region or nation. *Foreign tongue* means a language not of the person or persons being referenced. Page 4.

too _____ for words: to an extent that cannot adequately be described; extremely, as in *"too abused for words."* Used humorously. Page 122.

tooth and claw: variation of *tooth and nail*, to fight vigorously and fiercely with utmost effort and all one's might. Literally comes from biting and scratching with one's teeth and nails as weapons. Page 41.

to that effect: having that result, purpose or meaning. Page 133.

to the number of: at the quantity or amount of. Page 29.

tractable: easily managed or controlled. Page 89.

traffic officers: traffic policemen who control the smooth movement of automobiles, trucks, bicycles, etc., as at intersections, and ensure the safety of people who walk along or cross roads. Page 64.

transference: the act or process of being moved from one place to another. Page 111.

transplanted: literally (of a growing plant), dug up from one place and planted in another. Hence, brought from one region or country and settled in another; relocated. Page 38.

travails: efforts involving intense pain, agony and suffering. Page 31.

treatises: formal, usually extensive written works on a subject. Page 41.

treats (of): addresses or deals with. Page 65.

trial of a schoolteacher: a reference to the 1925 trial of John T. Scopes (1900–1970), a biology teacher in Dayton, Tennessee, USA, who by teaching the theory of evolution in his class, instead of the account of creation as given in the Bible, was accused of breaking the law. The trial received worldwide publicity and the press called it the Monkey Trial because, according to the theory of evolution, humans had descended from monkeys. Page 38.

trifle: to some small degree. Page 23.

triggered: initiated or set off; caused (some situation or condition) to happen as if acted on by a trigger. Page 105.

turmoil: a state of great confusion, disturbance and commotion. Page 38.

turn out to be: prove to be in the end; as is shown to be by (later) facts or events. Page 23.

turn (someone) like a top: a *top* is a round-shaped child's toy tapering to a steel point on which it can be made to spin. Hence, something that can *turn someone like a top*, can send a person into a spinning confusion. Page 66.

twine, mass of: *twine*, a strong string or cord made of two or more threads twisted together. A *mass of twine* is a cluster of tangled twine which is difficult to unravel. Page 17.

two-penny: of very little value, worthless. Page 75.

ugliness: ugliness is a disharmony in wave discord with theta. The description of ugliness and its use in auditing is contained in *Scientology 8-80. See also* **beauty**. Page 143.

unbeknownst: occurring or existing without the knowledge of; unperceived or unknown. Page 109.

underground: into hiding or secret operation as if beneath the surface of the earth. Page 89.

unprofitable: of no benefit or advantage; affords no improvement. Page 44.

unravel: to separate out and clarify the confusing elements of (something); make plain or clear; sort out. Literally, it means to undo or separate out entangled threads. Page 42.

unsavory: morally or socially objectionable or offensive; immoral. Page 5.

vagus nerve: either of the pair of nerves in the skull that convey impulses to the heart, lungs, stomach, intestines and various other organs. Page 104.

valence: an actual or shadow personality. One's own valence is his actual personality. Page 22.

Vedic: of or having to do with the Veda. The word *Veda* means *knowingness* or *sacred lore*. Page 38.

Vedic Hymns: the earliest learned writings of which we have any record on Earth. They are the most ancient sacred literature of the Hindus comprising over a hundred books still in existence. They tell about evolution, about Man coming into this universe and the curve of life which is birth, growth, degenerate and decay. Page 38.

very: used for emphasis with the meaning actual, as in *"the very breathing of their subjects."* Page 89.

vessel: literally, a hollow receptacle, as a cup, bowl, pitcher, etc., used for holding liquids or other contents. Hence, a body thought of as a *vessel*, a holder or container of something immaterial. Page 22.

vicarious: experienced through another person rather than firsthand. Page 131.

view, in plain: easily seen; clearly visible; noticeable. Page 27.

vindicate: to show that somebody or something is justified or correct. Page 37.

violence: 1. the exercise of physical force so as to inflict injury on, or cause damage to, persons or property, as in *"So overpoweringly awesome has been life on this line that the violence pervaded the social theory of psychology for decades."* Page 41.
2. great force; intensity and severity, as in *"If they are to be audited, they will react with violence—as much as a five- or twenty-dial drop on an E-Meter."* Page 43.

violently: in an extreme manner; very strongly or intensely. Page 5.

visio: the perceptic of sight, vision, in a mental image picture. Page 31.

volition: the power of choosing, deciding, exercising the will. Page 65.

voltage: the amount of pressure or force behind an electrical flow. Page 71.

voodooism: a body of beliefs and practices originally from Africa that includes magic and the supposed exercise of supernatural powers through the aid of evil spirits. Page 98.

waive: put aside or dismiss from consideration. Page 91.

war cry: literally, a cry or shout of troops in battle. Figuratively, it is something proclaimed to encourage a group to follow a course of action or principle. Page 64.

wavelength: a wavelength is a characteristic of motion. Many motions are too random, too chaotic to have orderly wavelengths. An orderly wavelength is a flow of motion. It has a regular repeated distance between its crests. Take a rope or the garden hose and give it a flip. You will see a wave travel along it. Energy—whether electrical, light or sound—has some such pattern.

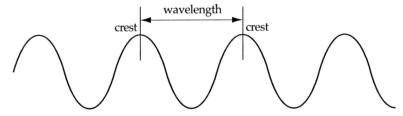

This is a smooth flowing wave. Its length is between crests. It is measured in units of length such as centimeters or inches or feet. Page 71.

wealth: a great amount or abundance of (something). Page 40.

Weeper: an incident on the genetic line. Described in Chapter Four. Page 40.

well-adjusted: in psychology, well adapted to one's environment, likening the individual to something (like a machine) that gets adjusted for different conditions or tasks. Page 115.

which is to say: a phrase used to introduce a clearer, more comprehensible, restatement of what immediately precedes or to limit or modify it. Page 42.

whole track: the entire track of the theta being beyond (earlier than) the present life. Page 4.

wide-open cases: cases which are possessed of full perception except somatic. *Wide-open* does not refer to a high-tone individual, but to one below 2.0 who *should* be easy to work but is often inaccessible and who finds it difficult to regain a somatic and simple to regain perception. The wide-open case is fully described in the lecture series *Technique 88: Incidents on the Track Before Earth.* Page 5.

widow-makers: persons or things which make widows by destroying husbands. Page 105.

wild: appearing or being manifested in an unexpected or unpredictable manner; random, erratic. Page 17.

wipe-out: a state or condition where the memory is knocked out, as in *"its cycle of birth, MEST body living, death, between-lives wipe-out and birth again."* Page 80.

wipe out: to knock out completely from the memory, as in *"To have been implanted once is to get a restimulation on dying which will wipe out the past life."* Page 110.

wipe (someone) out: to destroy or give a crushing defeat to, as in *"You can* really *wipe people out with electronics."* Page 89.

wise: way or manner. Page 91.

without number: of unknown or countless number; a large number. Page 64.

witness, as: used to introduce something that gives evidence of a fact or demonstrates a statement just made. Page 23.

wits, startled half out of their: frightened one extremely; *startled* means alarmed, frightened or surprised suddenly, and *wits* means one's mental composure or ability to think. Page 7.

woof and warp: variation of *warp and woof,* the basic material or foundation of a structure, entity, etc.; a reference to the threads that make up a woven fabric: the *warp* threads run lengthwise on the loom and the *woof* threads run crosswise. A *loom* is a frame or machine on which thread is woven into cloth. Page 17.

words, too _____ for: to an extent that cannot adequately be described; extremely, as in *"too abused for words."* Used humorously. Page 122.

workhorse: a person or thing that works tirelessly at a task without stopping. Originally the word applied to a horse used for labor, for pulling wagons, farming equipment, etc., as opposed to one used for riding or racing. Page 19.

work matters out: succeed in resolving something or bringing some effect about (through effort and work). Page 107.

work out: to accomplish the removal of by effort or action. Page 129.

wound up: arrived in a situation after or because of a course of action; ended up. Page 102.

wraps up: makes final; settles or brings to a successful conclusion. Page 6.

writers of the future: science-fiction writers are informally known as *writers of the future* because their stories deal with the future—time travel, space travel, life in other worlds, invasions of Earth, interplanetary warfare, etc. Page 90.

yearnings: deep longings or persistent desires for (something). Page 4.

yesterday (trained in): trained in the past; in this case past mental methods. Page 89.

yet: from the preceding time; as previously; still, as in *"their artifacts are yet in plain view."* Page 27.

yet (but), is: *yet* means as previously or still; *but* means merely or no more than; *yet but* means still only or no more than what has been mentioned, as in *"is yet but an animated vegetable."* Page 64.

yogism: the teachings of Yoga, a school of thought in the Hindu religion and a system of mental and physical exercise developed by that school. Page 97.

yokels: unpolished, naive or gullible inhabitants of a rural area or of a small town. Page 105.

Zeno: Greek philosopher (ca. 334–262 B.C.), who taught that it is foolish to try to shape circumstances to one's desires. One of the central themes of Zeno's philosophy was that Man should be free from passion and indifferent to emotion, pleasure and pain. It also taught that the universe was governed by divine will and happiness lay in conforming to such will. Page 64.

zephyr: a mild, gentle breeze. Page 66.

zombie: the body of a dead person given the similarity or appearance of life by an outside (usually evil) force. A zombie cannot speak and has no will. Page 65.

INDEX

genetic line, 37–57
  death marks progress, 44
  engrams, 19
  evolutionary chain on Earth, 12
  incidents, 43–57
  "past lives," 41
  what it consists of, 37
Glare Fights, 143
Greece, 41
Grim Weeper, 49
guilty, 92
gun
  half-light, half-black, 102

H

habit patterns, 4
half-light, half-black gun, 102
half-paralysis, 40, 102
Half-Transfer, 128
Halver, 101, 106
  basic under sexual
    malpractice, 103
  Blanketing and, 101
  description, 102
  religious symbols of, 103
Handbook for Preclears
  chart in, 90
Hearst weeklies, 74
heartbeat, 29
heavy facsimiles, 86
help
  failed, Misassist, 122
  get another low enough so he
    can be helped, 123
Helper, 39
  description, 45
  E-Meter and, 40
  mitosis incident, 45
  two sides to, 45
hide, desire to, 56

high aesthetic wave
  in auditing, 147
history
  study of, 41
Home Universe, 80
Homo novis, 62, 66
  limitations, 62
Homo sapiens, 62, 65
  above animals yet animal, 65
  composite, 64, 72
  thetans and, 74
"hot papa" suits, 105
How to Audit, 90
how to audit, 11–12
  two general problems in
    processing preclears
    see also **audit(ing)**, 11
human behavior, 17
hydrogen balloons, 21
hypnotic rapport, 53
hypnotic transference, 111
hypnotism, 22

I

"I", 128
  complete body control of, 115
  example of hydrogen
    balloons, 21
  fully alive as, 127
  identification of the real, 61
  theta being, 21
I Am, 90
Ice Cube, 108
identification
  real "I", 61
identification tags, 22
identity
  Concept Running and, 61
  confusion of, 21, 61, 130
  knowledge of, 72

basic error made, 102
behavior of, 132
body and, 138
decayed, 102
definition, 72
description, 73–74
drill to locate where the thetan
  is, 132
facsimiles and, 79
how to trap, 113
in-scan and out-scan, 138
liability to being, 130
lives his life in segments, 80
location of, 127–128
overt acts of, 81
somewhat bound-in here on
  Earth, 74
telepathy, 73
usual position, 138
war with MEST beings, 73
what it takes to aberrate a, 90
will need help and
  company, 74
see also **preclear; theta being**
theta-track incidents
  running, 85
Theta Trap Posts, 146
  basic of one having a body, 146
  see also **posts**
theta traps, 98, 113–116
  electronic force and, 113
  one thing in common, 113
  purpose, 113
Third Dynamic engrams, 46
thought, 11, 17, 85, 90
  independently of previous
    effort, counter-effort or
    experience, 21
thought, emotion and effort, 11,
72, 91
thought-police station, 90

thought transfer, 99
time
  thetan and, 73
time-space universes, 73
time track
  about 76 trillion years, 4
  case recovery and whole span
    of, 4
  collapse of, 100
  source of occlusion of, 100
  see also **whole track**
time warps, 73
Tone Scale
  charts, 17, 23
  perception and, 85
  theta beings activities and, 72
toothache, 18, 42, 47
tooth and claw, 41
Transfer, 127–132, 137, 138
  Control, 129
  Full, 128
  Half, 128
  Switch, 129
  Temporary versus
    Permanent, 128
traps, 98, 113–116
  definition, 113
  purpose, 113
trial of a schoolteacher, 38
tribal rebukes, 52
truth, 3
TV, 79

U

ugliness, beauty, 143, 147
unburdening, 86
unconsciousness, 63
universe
  only strong survive in, 63

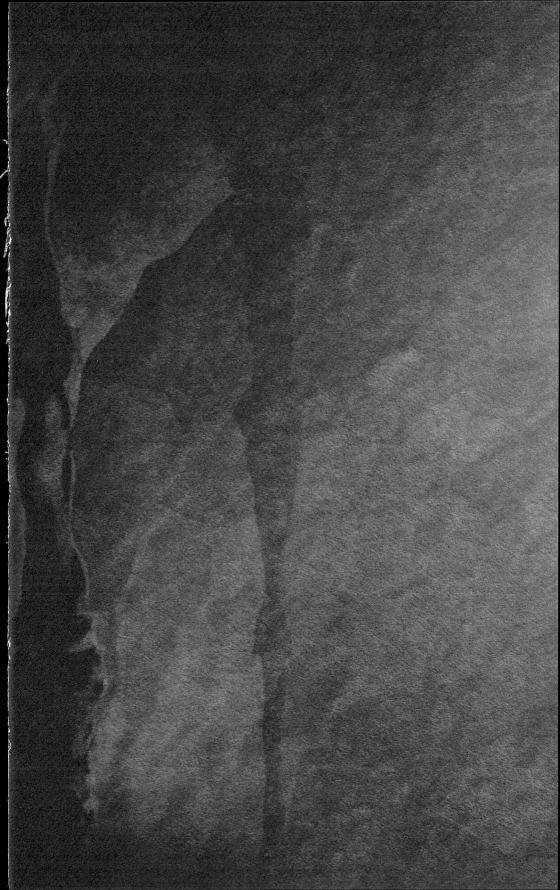

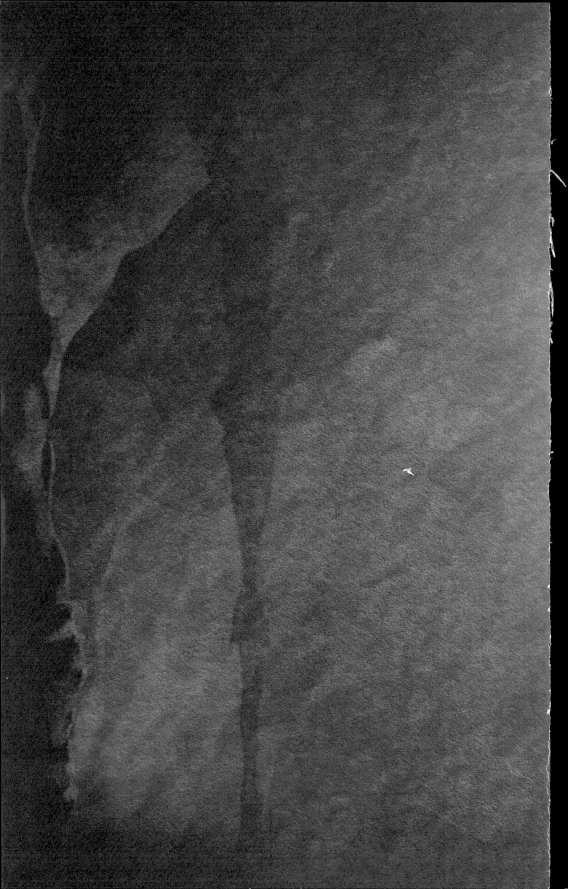